THE POLITICAL ECONOMY OF GOVERNMENT REGULATION

Topics in Regulatory Economics and Policy Series

Michael A. Crew, Editor
Graduate School of Management
Rutgers University
Newark, New Jersey, U.S.A.

Previously published books in the series:

Rowley, C., Tollison, R., and Tullock, G.:
  Political Economy of Rent-Seeking

Frantz, R.: *X-Efficiency*

Crew, M.: *Deregulation and Diversification
  of Utilities*

THE POLITICAL ECONOMY OF GOVERNMENT REGULATION

edited by
Jason F. Shogren
John A. Walker College of Business
Appalachian State University
Boone, North Carolina 28608 USA

Kluwer Academic Publishers
Boston/Dordrecht/London

Distributors for North America:
Kluwer Academic Publishers
101 Philip Drive
Assinippi Park
Norwell, Massachusetts 02061 USA

Distributors for all other countries:
Kluwer Academic Publishers Group
Distribution Centre
Post Office Box 322
3300 AH Dordrecht, THE NETHERLANDS

Library of Congress Cataloging-in-Publication Data

The Political economy of government regulation / edited by Jason F.
   Shogren.
         p.   cm. — (Topics in regulatory economics and policy series ;
   4)
     Papers presented at the 2nd annual Broyhill forum, held at and
   sponsored by Appalachian State University, Nov. 11, 1988.
     Includes index.
     ISBN 0-7923-9027-X
     1. Industry and state—Congresses.   2. Trade regulation-
   -Congresses.   I. Shogren, Jason F.   II. Appalachian State
   University.   III. Series: Topics in regulatory economics and policy
   ; 4.
   HD3612.P65   1989
   338.9—dc20   89-33779
                                                                CIP

Printed in the United States of America

To Maija

Contents

Acknowledgements   ix

Contributors   xi

1 Introduction and Overview   1
  Jason F. Shogren

2 Political Competition Among Interest Groups   13
  Gary S. Becker

3 Bootleggers and Baptists in the Market for   29
  Regulation
  Bruce Yandle

4 Partial Regulation of Natural Monopoly   55
  John Tschirhart

5 The Political Economy of Risk Communication   83
  Policies for Food and Alcoholic Beverages
  W. Kip Viscusi

6 Economic Prescriptions for Environmental   131
  Problems: Not Exactly What the Doctor Ordered
  Robert W. Hahn

7 Disclosure, Consent, and Environmental Risk   191
  Regulation
  F. Reed Johnson

ACKNOWLEDGEMENTS

The chapters is this volume originated from the second annual Broyhill Forum on Economic Issues entitled "Perspectives on Government Regulation" at Appalachian State University on November 11, 1988. The forum was sponsored by the University and by a grant from the Broyhill Foundation. I want to thank Dean Paul Combs, Chairman Larry Ellis, and Professors Steve Millsaps, Garey Durden, Tim Perri, and Fred Wallace for their support. I am indebted to the distinguished speakers for their cooperation in making the forum a success and this book possible. Finally, Deborah Culler once again provided valuable assistance in the preparation of the manuscript.

CONTRIBUTING AUTHORS

Gary S. Becker is the University Professor of Economics and Sociology at the University of Chicago. He received his Ph.D. from the University of Chicago in 1955. Professor Becker received the John Bates Clark Medal in 1967, and has been President of the American Economic Association (1987). He is a Fellow of the Econometric Society and the American Academy of Arts and Sciences. In addition, Professor Becker is a Member of the National Academy of Sciences and the Domestic Advisory Board for the Hoover Institution.

Robert W. Hahn is a Senior Staff Economist for the U.S. Council of Economic Advisors and Associate Professor of Economics at Carnegie-Mellan University. He received his Ph.D. from the California Institute of Technology in 1981. Dr. Hahn has received the Barr Award for outstanding research in applied public economics and a Brookings Fellowship.

F. Reed Johnson is Associate Professor of Economics at the U.S. Naval Academy and Intermittent Expert for the Office of Policy at the U.S. Environmental Protection Agency. He received his Ph.D. from State University of New York, Stony Brook in 1974. Professor Johnson has been a Fulbright-Hayes Scholar in 1973 and 1984, and a Brookings Economic Policy Fellow in 1978.

Jason F. Shogren is Assistant Professor of Economics and Director of the Broyhill Forum on Economic Issues (1988-89) at Appalachian State University. He received his Ph.D. from the University of Wyoming in 1986.

John Tschirhart is Professor of Law and Economics at the University of Wyoming. He received his Ph.D. from Purdue University in 1975. Professor Tschirhart has been a Teaching Fellow at Australian National University.

W. Kip Viscusi is the George G. Allen Professor of Economics at Duke University. He received his Ph.D. from Harvard University in 1976. Professor Viscusi has been John M. Olin Visiting Professor of Economics at the University of Chicago in 1985 and Deputy Director of the President's Council on Wage and Price Stability in 1979-1981. Currently, he is a Research Associate for the National Bureau of Economic Research and Co-editor of the Journal of Risk and Uncertainty.

Bruce Yandle is the Alumni Professor of Economics at Clemson University. He received his Ph.D. from Georgia State University in 1970. Professor Yandle has been Executive Director of the U.S. Federal Trade Commission in 1982, Adjunct Scholar for the American Enterprise Institution since 1978, and Senior Economist for the President's Council on Wage and Price Stability in 1976.

THE POLITICAL ECONOMY OF GOVERNMENT REGULATION

1
INTRODUCTION AND OVERVIEW
Jason F. Shogren

My education in the political economy of
regulation began when I auctioned off a one dollar
bill for $25. The rules of the auction are
simple, the results illustrative. The highest
bidder receives the dollar, pays nothing; the
second highest bidder must pay his bid but
receives nothing; and all bidders are constrained
to their budget. Try it sometime, the auction
never fails to generate bids exceeding one
dollar.[1]

The auction illustrates the dependence of the
market system on the rules and regulations which
define that system. Although price is the
allocation mechanism, market outcomes are
contingent on the regulations which define
property rights. The implication is that the
individuals or groups which control or influence
the regulatory environment determine the
distribution of wealth even in a free market
economy (see Plott 1986). The auction ended my
naive view of the separation between prices and
rules; government regulation in a market economy
requires the integration of economic efficiency
with political reality.

Each chapter in this volume presents a unique view of the political economy of government regulation. The volume originated out of the second annual Broyhill Forum on Economic Issues at Appalachian State University.[2] In November of 1988, the one-day conference entitled "Perspectives on Government Regulation" provided a forum for the group of six prominent economists featured in this book. The purpose of this volume is to provide a permanent record of their views and insights. The reader of this book should come away with a good idea of the variety of current approaches to the political economy of regulation.

Chapter 2, by Gary Becker, explores the economic theory of regulation. The economic theory of regulation as developed by Stigler (1971) and extended by Peltzman (1976) and Becker (1983) examines whether political outcomes are influenced by powerful interest groups and, if so, what are the various avenues and dimensions of influence. Becker further develops his argument that political competition between interest groups may prove a useful means of providing more efficient regulation. Efficiency is promoted through competition since groups receiving large subsidies stimulate countervailing pressure by those groups taxed to finance the subsidies. A regulation that produces gains rather than dead weight costs is more likely to be adopted and survive since the group which captures the gain has the comparative advantage relative to those that are harmed. Becker's main conclusion is that competition between interest groups tends to correct market failure and minimize dead weight losses in the process of wealth redistribution.

Becker's view of interest groups stands in stark contrast to another economic theory of regulation: the public choice approach (Buchanan and Tullock 1962). The public choice theory of regulation as developed by Olson (1982) argues that interest group competition introduces

significant bias into political markets by
diverting resources from efficient allocation.
Olson argues that as a society remains stable for
long periods, interest groups accumulate which are
more concerned with distributional struggles than
production. The process is equivalent to
wrestlers battling over the contents in a china
shop, breaking more than they carry away (Olson
1988). Olson concludes that the accumulation of
interest group coalitions will lead to
productivity slowdowns, sluggish growth, and
eventually, the decline of a nation.

Becker challenges Olson's view that long-stable
societies should be less efficient and dynamic
than comparative societies that have had no time
to accumulate coalitions. Becker argues that if
the public choice approach is correct then one
would expect low growth in democratic societies
with open and intense competition among interest
groups. He describes preliminary evidence which
indicates that per capita income growth is
positively, not negatively, related to the degree
of political democracy. Becker concludes that
nothing in these results implies that political
democracy with keen interest group competition is
harmful to growth.

The next chapter, by Bruce Yandle, presents a
theory of interest group behavior which quantifies
Charles Dudley Warner's famous remark "politics
makes strange bedfellows." Yandle's theory of
bootleggers and Baptists differs from Becker in
that coordinated, not competing, interest groups
are examined. An uneasy coalition between rent-
seeking bootleggers and public-interest minded
Baptists is forged to promote regulation that
satisfies both parties. As an example, Yandle
describes how both parties gain from the Sunday
closings of the corner liquor store. The
bootleggers gain from decreased competition, while
the Baptists gain from reduced indirect
competition and diminished consumption of

alcoholic beverages.

In developing his model Yandle revives the public interest theory of regulation; the view that regulation is designed for the good of all in which regulators strive to maximize social welfare. Yandle's use of the public interest theory is not a naive reintroduction, but rather a reconstruction with a sinister twist. The public interest theory with its moral content acts as a smoke screen to conceal highly visible special interest benefits. Politicians and regulators can justify their actions as defending the public interest, thereby sidestepping obvious benefits to special interests.

Yandle presents four regulatory episodes to illustrate his theory: State regulation of Sunday retail sales (Blue laws), federal regulation of flammable sleepwear, state regulation of gambling and lottery laws, and state/federal regulation of seatbelts and airbags. Yandle points out that in those cases where the bootleggers lose the moral content of the Baptists, the regulation can and will die. The importance of this result is that coordinated interest groups with the same means to different ends creates the potential for cross subsidization. In regulatory episodes that are highly controversial, there may be incentive for the rent-seeking bootleggers to subsidize the public-interest Baptists. The subsidy would provide an indirect moral avenue for rent-seeking behavior, thereby lowering the political costs of supporting the regulation. Optimal subsidization would increase the difficulty of empirically identifying rent-seeking from the public interest motive. Future empirical tests of the economic theory of regulation should consider Yandle's model when attempting to identify the various avenues of political influence (also see Nowell and Tschirhart 1988).

Chapter 3, by John Tschirhart, explores the implications of partial regulation. Specifically,

Tschirhart is concerned with the undesirable
consequences of partially regulating a multiproduct natural monopoly. The study of partial
regulation is extremely timely given the
deregulation and diversification movement of the
past decade. The rapidly changing regulatory
environment has led to firms operating in both
regulated and competitive markets. Industries
affected by deregulation include trucking,
airlines, telecommunications, public utilities,
and banking (see Crew 1989). The result is that
both regulators and firms are struggling with
problems such as how to avoid cross subsidies
between regulated and unregulated markets and when
to encourage or discourage entry into markets.
     Tschirhart develops a framework for examining
the consequences of partially regulating a natural
monopoly by incorporating the idea of
sustainability. Sustainability exists if a firm
can charge a price for output that will block
competitive entry (Panzer and Willig 1977).
Tschirhart demonstrates three undesirable
consequences of partial regulation. First, if a
firm is a natural monopoly, then its partially
regulated prices will be sustainable and economic
profits will be positive (profits in excess of
opportunity cost). Second, if a totally regulated
multi-product firm is a nonsustainable natural
monopoly, whether the firm becomes sustainable
under partial regulation depends upon which
markets are deregulated. Cross subsidization to
support sustainability may also occur. Third, a
partially regulated non-natural monopoly can be
sustainable due to cross subsidization of the
unregulated market. All three results are
unpredicted by models of total regulation or total
deregulation, and exist from the inability of
regulators to accurately allocate common costs
across multiple products (also see Sherman 1989).
     Tschirhart's analysis demonstrates that the
transition from total regulation to partial

deregulation can lead to undesirable results. He
qualifies his results, however, by pointing out
three main caveats to the model: the assumptions
of optimal regulatory policies, costlessly
implemented regulation, and constant technology.
By highlighting the caveats, Tschirhart has
pointed out the future research directions in an
area ripe for further exploration.

The next chapter, by W. Kip Viscusi, introduces
the focus of the remainder of the volume:
environmental regulation in a market economy.
Viscusi examines the efficacy and political
context of risk communication policies for food
and alcoholic beverages. Risk communication
policies or hazard warnings are an attractive
alternative to current standard-setting
approaches.

Viscusi proposes six principles for developing
effective hazard warning policies. The principles
are based on how individuals process risk
information and make decisions under uncertainty.
Understanding how decisions are made in risky
situations will determine the information content
of hazard warnings. Obtaining and processing
information are costly activities, however. Since
an individual's ability to process information is
limited, more information may confuse rather than
improve decision making. Studies confirm that a
limit exists beyond which additional information
does not improve decisions. Magat et al. (1988)
demonstrate that hazard warnings can be effective,
but the cognitive limitations of individuals are
important. Increasing the amount of risk
information creates an information processing
trade-off. Individuals recall less information
due to problems of information overload. Viscusi
concludes that information contained in hazard
warnings can be effective, but content must be
carefully designed to account for an individual's
information processing abilities (also see Smith
et al. 1988).

Viscusi also reviews the institutional context
of hazard warning programs for federally-proposed
alcohol beverage warning legislation and food
cancer warnings in the State of California.
Viscusi argues the language of the hazard warnings
maximize political interests rather than advancing
the primary objective of informing consumers and
enabling them to make better decisions. By
ignoring fundamental economic and psychological
concepts of decision-making under risk, the
currently-proposed warnings do not convey the
information necessary for consumers to make sound
choices regarding risks and precautions. Both
warning programs, however, do provide an excellent
opportunity to incorporate Viscusi's principles
for effective hazard warning policies.

Chapter 6, by Robert Hahn, presents a detailed
examination of the economic approach to
environmental reform. Hahn explores the economics
and politics of two alternative mechanisms which
use pricing incentives to attain a given
environmental standard: marketable permits and
emission charges. A marketable permit system
allows well-defined, tradeable property right
permits for environmental resources to be
auctioned off to the highest bidder. In an
emission charge system, the state sets a fixed
price for each unit of pollution, and then allows
each firm to optimally select its level of
discharge. In contrast to the traditional
environmental strategy of command and control,
both marketable permits and emission charges
satisfy the criterion of economic efficiency; they
minimize cost to society.

Hahn details the actual experience of several
European countries and the United States with
marketable permits and emission charges. By
focusing on the actual implementation of the
economic approaches, Hahn highlights the
divergence between theory and the performance of
the mechanisms. The divergence arises because

economists have generally not addressed the
political environment in which the mechanisms are
selected and implemented. Hahn stresses the need
for a more general theory of environmental
regulation which incorporates the political forces
shaping the new economic approaches.

In describing a more complete theory of
environmental reform, Hahn challenges Becker's
theory of interest group competition. Recall,
Becker argues that regulatory efficiency will be
increased due to keen competition among opposing
interest groups. Hahn questions Becker's theory
by asking why we have not seen the wide-spread
implementation of the mechanisms which promote
economic efficiency. For example, marketable
permits have existed in theory since Crocker's
(1966) initial model. However, political pressure
has been insufficient to promote implementation.
Whether efficient, market-oriented approaches to
environmental regulation will eventually be
adopted remains to be seen.

The final chapter, by F. Reed Johnson, examines
some practical and ethical dilemmas confronting
regulators charged with protecting public health
from environmental risk. Johnson treats the
regulator as the provider of information on the
nature of the risk. Two alternative information
programs are considered: the traditional
standard-setting approach of disclosure and the
economic-based approach of informed consent. The
disclosure approach imposes expert opinion about
what policies are most appropriate to protect
public health. The approach attempts to minimize
the incidence of morbidity and mortality in the
population by constructing a uniform threshold of
acceptable risk. In contrast, the information
policy of informed consent reflects the principle
of respect for individual autonomy. Given
preferences for risk vary substantially in a
population, informed consent limits government's
role to disseminating information in a form most

useful to the individual. The individual then
selects a level of protection based on risk
preferences.

As shown by Tversky and Kahneman (1981),
however, individual responses to risk are subject
to the framing and presentation of information.
Like Viscusi, Johnson stresses that regulators
should pay as much attention to _how_ they provide
the information as to _what_ information they
provide. Recent work on the information content
of pamphlets describing the risks associated with
radon have demonstrated that information
disclosure based on standard-setting assumptions
yield significantly different perceptions and
behavior relative to those based on informed
consent assumptions (see Smith et al. 1988).

Disclosure and consent raise the issue of ex
ante/ex post choice in welfare theory under
uncertainty. Standard welfare theory aggregates
individual preferences to obtain a social welfare
function. Under uncertainty, the social welfare
function can be derived in two ways: ex ante and
ex post states of the world. An ex ante choice
implies deriving a social welfare function by
maximizing individual expected utility (using
individual perception of risk) and summing the
individual benefits. The ex post choice derives a
social welfare function by summing individual
preferences and maximizing aggregate expected
welfare (using expert perception of risk).
Hammond (1981) demonstrates that the ex ante and
the ex post approaches will be equivalent if and
only if (i) all individuals have the same
perception of risk, equal to the regulator, and
(ii) the social welfare function is a weighted sum
of individual utilities.

A social welfare function should respect
individual preferences. However, Sandmo (1983)
points out that although preferences are usually
assumed synonymous with "tastes," the regulator
might not respect individual (mis)perceptions of

risk. The regulator must decide whether to use
individual perceptions (ex ante) or use his own
perception (ex post) derived from expert opinion.

Suppose experts argue that a risk from a
certain product is acceptable, but the public does
not. Does the regulator ban the product or allow
individuals to use their own discretion? The
dilemma is to balance the tradeoff between
preserving individual freedom of choice and
maintaining public safety. The regulator may be
tempted to regulate the risk in the best interest
of society. Such paternalistic action, however,
conflicts with our society's commitment to
consumer sovereignty--the individual is best able
to judge what is in his or her own self interest.
These important ethical questions raised by
Johnson's chapter undoubtedly will dominate the
regulation of environmental risk for a long time
to come.

Beyond exploring the current state of research
in several areas, I hope this volume will enliven
the dialogue between the practitioners and
students of regulation. By collecting various
views, our goal is to provide a book that on the
whole is more than the sum of its parts; with each
direction explored increasing our understanding of
the political economy of government regulation.

Notes

1. I first saw the auction demonstrated by Charles Plott. Plott also provided
the real life parallel to the auction. Consider the payment schedule in legal
actions. The payment structure is often set so the losing party pays for both his
own legal fees and those of the winning party. The winning party pays nothing.
The incentive is for both parties to hire the best legal council money can buy.
The resulting legal fees often exceed the dollar value of the original complaint.

2. The first Broyhill Forum in 1987 was entitled "Economic and Political
Perspectives on the Federal Budget Deficit." The featured speakers included James
Buchanan, Robert Barro, and Senator Terry Sanford. See Ellis and Millsaps (1988).

References

Baumol, William J. and Wallace E. Oates, The Theory of Environmental Policy, Second Edition, Cambridge: Cambridge University Press, 1988.

Becker, Gary S., "A Theory of Competition Among Pressure Groups for Political Influence," Quarterly Journal of Economics 98 (1983): 371-400.

Buchanan, James and Gordon Tullock, The Calculus of Consent, Ann Arbor: University of Michigan Press, 1962.

Crew, Michael A., editor, Deregulation and Diversification of Utilities, Norwell, Mass.: Kluwer Academic Publishers, 1989.

Crocker, Thomas D., "The Structuring of Atmospheric Pollution Control Systems," in The Economics of Air Pollution, edited by H. Wolozing, New York: W. W. Norton, 1966, 61-86.

Ellis, Larry V. and Steve W. Millsaps, editors, Perspectives on the Federal Budget Deficit, Boone, NC: Appalachian Consortium Press, 1988.

Hammond, Peter, "Ex-Ante and Ex-Post Welfare Optimality under Uncertainty," Economica 50 (1981): 19-33.

Magat, Wesley A., W. Kip Viscusi, and Joel Huber, "Consumer Processing of Hazard Warning Information," Journal of Risk and Uncertainty 1 (1988): 201-232.

Nowell, Clifford and John Tschirhart, "Testing Competing Theories of Regulatory Behavior," Paper presented at the American Economic Association Meeting, New York 1988.

Olson, Mancur, The Rise and Decline of Nations: Economic Growth, Stagflation, and Social Rigidities, New Haven: Yale University Press, 1982.

_____, "The Productivity Slowdown, the Oil Shocks, and the Real Cycle," Journal of Economic Perspectives 2 (1988): 43-69.

Panzer, John C. and Robert D. Willig, "Free Entry

and the Sustainability of Natural Monopoly,"
Bell Journal of Economics 8 (1977): 1-22.

Peltzman, Sam, "Towards a More General Theory of
Regulation," Journal of Law and Economics 19
(1976): 211-240.

Plott, Charles, "Laboratory Experiments in
Economics: The Implications of Posted-Price
Institutions," Science 232 (1986): 732-738.

Sandmo, A., "Ex-Post Welfare Economics and the
Theory of Merit Goods," Economica 50 (1983):
19-33.

Sherman, Roger, "Efficiency Aspects of
Diversification by Public Utilities," in
Deregulation and Diversification of Utilities,
edited by Michael A. Crew, Norwell, Mass.:
Kluwer Academic Publishers, 1989, 43-63.

Smith, V. Kerry, William H. Desvouges, Ann Fisher,
and F. Reed Johnson, "Learning about Radon's
Risk," Journal of Risk and Uncertainty 1
(1988): 233-258.

Stigler, George J., "The Theory of Economic
Regulation," Bell Journal of Economics 2
(1971): 3-21.

Tversky, Amos and Daniel Kahneman, "The Framing of
Decisions and the Psychology of Choice,"
Science 211 (1981): 453-458.

2

POLITICAL COMPETITION AMONG INTEREST GROUPS
Gary S. Becker

Selfishness in the Marketplace[1]

Let me start with a quotation familiar to some of you: "It is not from the benevolence of the butcher, the brewer, or the baker that we expect our dinner, but from their regard to their own interest." The same author went on to say with some irony, "We are not ready to suspect any person of being defective in selfishness." These are statements by Adam Smith, the founder of modern economics. The first statement is from the greatest book ever written on economics, called The Wealth of Nations, the second from a good book called The Theory of Moral Sentiments.

Smith was not stating that he thought people should be selfish, as argued in certain modern philosophies, but was assessing how people typically are motivated. However, he did develop a different type of normative analysis. In a remarkable argument he showed that under appropriate conditions, it does not matter that people are selfish. For a selfish person, and I quote the most famous statement in The Wealth of Nations, "intends only his own gain and he is in this as in many other cases led by an invisible hand to promote an end which was no part of his intention. By pursuing his own interest he

frequently promotes that of the society more
effectively than when he really intends to promote
it." How can such an optimistic statement at the
very beginning of the science be reconciled with
the claim that economics is "the dismal science?"

In an important sense, Smith can be said to
have shown how societies can economize on love,
that very scarce "resource." Smith was not happy
that people are selfish; he wished that people
were more altruistic. But he was hardheaded and a
scientist, and accepted people the way they are.
Since people are generally selfish, societies
cannot be organized around love. Fortunately,
however, he was able to show that selfish people,
under appropriate conditions, are led by this
invisible hand to promote the public interest. In
other words, it is not necessary to have much
altruism when selfish persons can be induced to
act as if they are altruistic toward others.

His argument should be familiar since it has
been elaborated by the economics profession during
the last two hundred years. If some firms are not
promoting the public interest--if they are making
excessive profits--he argued that other firms
would start competing against them (if permitted
to compete), and this would lower market prices
until they equalled costs. Similarly, if firms
could sell at a higher price in one geographical
area than in another area, they would ship goods
to the area where they could sell at the higher
price, lowering the price there and raising the
price in the first area. Moreover, workers free
to change jobs would leave low paying jobs or
those with poor working conditions and compete for
the better jobs. Their competition equalizes
wages and conditions in different jobs. And so on
for other market adjustments.

Smith rightly emphasized that the "invisible
hand" requires freedom to enter and exit from
industries, jobs, and consumer products. It also
assumes that government intervention does not

prevent competitive prices from emerging. Smith's
analysis of competition has been maintained
unchanged in modern economics except for the
development of a more sophisticated and complete
analysis of the conditions when self-interest
promotes the general welfare.

One prominent condition is the absence of
direct interactions between people or between
firms and people. They interact, for example,
when firms spew smoke into surrounding
neighborhoods, as steel mills in Gary, Indiana
pollute the area of Chicago where I live (although
the air has become clearer as the domestic steel
industry encountered bad times). Firms usually do
not take account of the harmful effects they
impose on others unless forced to do so. Another
condition is that transactions must be feasible.
The cost of transacting cannot be large enough to
prevent mutually profitable and mutually
beneficial transactions. Smith's conclusion does
not follow when there are direct interactions or
large transaction costs, and selfish behavior may
not promote the general welfare.

Selfishness in the Political Sector

It is natural to look to governments to offset
the harmful effects of selfish behavior. Adam
Smith himself advocated a significant government
role. These included protection against foreign
aggression and domestic crime, the enforcement of
contracts, and the provision of education.

During the first half of the twentieth century,
economists usually assumed that governments are
benevolent. Governments were believed to act to
control the effects of direct interactions and
transactions costs, and to tax income and wealth
to achieve an ethically sound distribution of
resources. Our founding fathers, however, had a
more skeptical and realistic view of government.
They knew that governments can be oppressive, and

that governments often cater to powerful special
interests. The founding fathers tried to design a
constitution and other procedures that would limit
oppression and the power of special interests, and
yet would permit governments to carry out tasks
that could not be handled well privately.

Economists have also begun during the past
thirty years to take a more realistic view of
government behavior. The considerable analytic
artillery of modern economics is being used to
develop an understanding of how governments
actually behave. I would like to sketch out some
of the conclusions and insights that have been
obtained.

Governments do not automatically solve the
problems created by selfish behavior in the
marketplace primarily because bureaucrats,
legislators, and voters also tend to be selfish,
and seek to promote their own interests. After
all, participants in the political sector are the
same kind of people as participants in the private
sector. Although the power and force at the
disposal of modern governments can be channeled
toward useful purposes, they can also be channeled
toward the enrichment of powerful groups at the
expense of weak groups that sometimes include a
large majority of the population. As a result,
government actions frequently worsen rather than
improve the outcomes of private markets.

To take a common example, agricultural
interests in the United States and other Western
countries have used their political power to lower
the production and raise the prices of sugar,
tobacco, grains, milk, and other products through
acreage restrictions, limits on imports, payments
that require land to remain uncultivated, and in
many other ways. Moreover, government assistance
to agriculture has become more extensive during
the past forty years as farming has shrunk to a
small part of the modern economy.

Therefore, to understand what governments

actually do, as opposed to what they ought to do,
it is necessary to understand how selfish groups
with special interests influence political
outcomes. I will discuss a few implications of an
analysis of political pressure groups that I
develop elsewhere in more detail (see Becker 1983,
1985a).

Competition Among Pressure Groups

Successful pressure groups are often small.
Although sometimes there is the tyranny of the
majority feared by opponents of democracy, more
frequently well-disciplined small groups wield
political power. Small groups are successful
politically when they are well organized, and can
persuade many voters and legislators to support
them.

Although fewer than 11,000 farms produce sugar
in the United States, they--along with producers
of corn sweeteners--have raised the demand for
domestic sugar by inducing the Federal government
to restrict imports from countries (many in the
Caribbean) with more efficient producers of sugar.
The domestic price of sugar is now about four
times the world price (20¢ per pound compared to
less than 5¢ per pound). Similarly, the
automobile industry in the United States only has
four producers and fewer than 800,000 workers, yet
the Chrysler Corporation managed to obtain a
sizable subsidy when on the verge of bankruptcy,
and the industry has been successful in getting
tariffs and quotas placed on cars produced by more
efficient Japanese firms.

The methods that small groups use to obtain the
support of others are varied, but frequently
include propaganda and highly misleading claims.
Voters are vulnerable to persuasion because they
do not have much incentive to become well informed
about political issues since each voter has only a
minor effect on political outcomes that are

decided by the majority or by similar rules.
Therefore, the average person knows far more about
supermarket prices and the performance of cars
than about import quotas and public wages.
Although rational political behavior has appeared
to be contradicted by widespread voter ignorance
and apathy, the opposite conclusions is warranted
because rational voters do not want to invest much
in political information.

Doctors, the military complex, and other groups
who contribute to defense, nationalism,
conservation, health, and other popular goods
often can elicit political support because it is
easier to promote interests that are generally
believed to contribute to popular goals.
Moreover, research findings that oppose the
interests of powerful pressure groups frequently
have little political impact because they are
offset by the dissemination of misinformation and
by other appeals to public opinion and
legislatures.

Special interest groups are often successful
politically even when their subsidies are financed
by sizable taxes on other groups. However, those
paying taxes are sometimes stimulated to organize
and to lobby for lower taxes, and hence for lower
public support to the groups who are subsidized by
their taxes. This inducement to organize is a
form of "countervailing power" that limits the
power of pressure groups.

The potential for countervailing power implies
that groups are more likely to be successful
politically when the taxes on others are not large
relative to their subsidies. Then even if the
groups harmed did organize, they might spend less
to promote lower taxes than the groups benefited
would spend to promote higher subsidies. This is
why crackpot proposals that greatly reduce
aggregate wealth do not usually muster enough
support: the political opposition is simply too
powerful.

Dead Weight Costs and Political Power

The new welfare economics developed the
compensation principle to determine whether public
policies are socially beneficial. Some of the
pioneers even claimed that a policy is beneficial
as long as gainers <u>could</u> compensate losers,
regardless of whether compensation were actually
paid. This view is untenable except when the
political process has equalized the marginal
social "worths" of gainers and losers, which begs
the question of what determines <u>actual</u> policies.
Nevertheless, distribution continues to be
neglected by most assessments of the harm from
monopoly and other "market failures," and by most
evaluations of public policies; these essentially
consider only whether gainers <u>could</u> compensate
losers.

Yet, somewhat paradoxically, the potential to
compensate is an important determinant of <u>actual</u>
political behavior in a model of competing
interest groups. The reason is that the maximum
expenditure by gainers to support a policy would
exceed the maximum expenditure by losers to oppose
the policy if, and only if, the sum of the
monetary equivalents of the gains and losses to
all persons were positive. An increase in the sum
of these monetary equivalents will be called an
increase in "social output." The link between
social output and incentives to exert pressure
does not presume that pressure groups are
altruistic, nor that compensation is paid to
losers, nor that any social welfare function is
politically relevant, for they are linked even in
a noncooperative game without side payments
between competing and selfish pressure groups.

If the monetary equivalents of the gains were
smaller than the monetary equivalents of the
losses, a policy would not be implemented unless
gainers had much better access to political
influence. Therefore, the compensation principle

combined with an analysis of the production of
political influence provides a unified approach to
the political feasibility both of public goods and
other policies that raise social output (where
gains are large enough to compensate losses), and
of policies that redistribute to favored groups
(where gains are too small to compensate).

The emphasis in the theory on dead weight costs
is reminiscent of Ramsey pricing and the theory of
optimal taxation, where marginal dead weight costs
are related to marginal "social worths." However,
optimal tax theory uses dead weight costs to
prescribe optimal public policies, whereas my
analysis uses dead weight costs to explain actual
policies in a world of competing and possibly
selfish pressure groups. Still, if dead weight
cost (and benefits) are important determinants of
actual policies, the many calculations of dead
weight cost in the applied welfare literature, and
many analytical results of welfare economics and
optimal tax theory, are relevant also to positive
theories of political behavior.

The rapid growth of government regulations and
government expenditures in the late 1950s, 1960s,
and most of the 1970s seemed unstoppable.
Government was modeled as a Leviathan with an
insatiable appetite (see Brennan and Buchanan
1984). But then to everyone's surprise, the
"deregulation movement" began in the United States
and spread to other countries. This movement
involved the removal of government regulations in
the airline and several other industries. In
addition, the highest marginal income tax rates
were sharply cut in the United States, Great
Britain, Israel, and elsewhere, and government
owned enterprises were sold off in a worldwide
clamor for "privatization."

Is a rational model of competition among
political pressure groups more successful than the
Leviathan model in explaining these remarkable
developments? I believe the answer is "yes"

because of the crucial role of dead weight costs
in models of political competition. Deregulation
of airlines, banks, security firms, and other
industries in the United States is largely
consistent with the implication of an analysis
where political support for a regulation withers
when its dead weight cost becomes large.

Dead weight costs of regulations and other
policies often rise over time as labor and capital
become more mobile, as substitutes develop for
products that have been made more expensive, and
as other costly methods of evading and avoiding
the effects of particular regulations are
discovered. The dead weight cost of regulating
security transactions did rise significantly over
time as institutional investors with elastic
demands became important (see Jarrell 1984). The
cost of regulating airline travel rose as airline
travel expanded into new and diverse markets (see
Spiller 1983), and as nonprice competition greatly
reduced profit margins (see Peltzman 1988). The
social cost of the 1970s' banking regulations grew
as interest rates became higher and more variable
during the worldwide inflation, and as new methods
of intermediation were invented (Carron 1983).

Microwave technology and the rents built into
the long distance telephone price structure
stimulated the growth of MCI and other companies
that used this technology to provide opportunities
for communication among business users. This
competition destroyed the rents to AT&T from long
distance calls and led to the demise of its
regulatory monopoly (Peltzman 1988). The dead
weight cost of high marginal income tax grew as
tax shelters, the underground economy, and other
"loop-holes" were expanded.

By 1980 regulation of railroads and trucking
through the ICC had virtually ended. The
abolition of railroad rate regulation is not
surprising because the growth of trucking and air
freight provided close and politically powerful

substitutes. But the end of practically all
interstate trucking regulation is puzzling and not
readily consistent with models of pressure group
competition.[2]
     Nor is it easy for the theory to explain the
accelerated growth in recent years of other
regulations, especially those affecting labor
markets and environmental use. For example, not
long ago, employers were more or less free to hire
and fire "at will," whereas now they are subject
to suits charging discrimination by age, sex, and
race, invasion of privacy, and other "unfair"
behavior. These developments are not an accident
of politics in the United States, for they are
found in essentially all Western nations.

Democracy and Efficiency

     The almost universal condemnation of special
interest groups includes the recent allegation by
Olson (1982) that they are responsible for
sluggish growth and the eventual decline of
nations. Most of the condemnation is based on the
many redistributions to special interest groups
that reduce social output because of dead weight
costs of taxes and subsidies.
     However, actual political systems do not have
social welfare functions, benevolent dictators, or
other political procedures that <u>automatically</u>
choose the optimal production of public goods,
optimal effluence taxes, and other public policies
that raise output and efficiency. Therefore, the
condemnation of special interest groups is
excessive because competition among these groups
contributes to the survival of policies that raise
social output: favorably affected groups tend to
lobby more for these policies than unfavorably
affected groups lobby against since the former
tend to gain more than the latter lose. Indeed,
no policy that lowered social output would survive
if all groups were equally large and skillful at

producing political influence, for the opposition
would always exert more influence than proponents.

The condemnation of special interest groups is
more justified when there is highly unequal access
to political influence. Powerful groups then can
secure the implementation of policies that benefit
them while reducing social output, and can thwart
policies that harm them while raising output.

If special interest groups are crucial to the
political process, political systems would be
largely defined by their activities and
opportunities. Democracies have competition among
groups with highly unequal strength.
Redistribution in democracies (and other systems)
would be guided not by social welfare functions or
other measures of social fairness, but mainly by
the altruism, selfishness, envy, and morality of
the more powerful interest groups.

In democracies so defined, a few pressure
groups cannot easily obtain very large subsidies
(although many groups may each obtain relatively
small subsidies), since I have shown that large
subsidies stimulate countervailing pressure by
those taxed to finance the subsidies. In
totalitarian systems, on the other hand, a few
groups can more readily use the state to raise
substantially their well-being because other
groups are not permitted to form effective
opposition.

I reflected on these issues during a recent
trip to the Far East. Korea, Taiwan, and Hong
Kong have all done extremely well economically
without having many political freedoms.
Businessmen there are worried about the effect on
economic growth of the trend toward political
democracy--even Hong Kong residents are electing a
legislature that is supposed to retain many powers
after the takeover by China in 1997. But the
qualitative evidence from many countries on the
relation between growth and democracy provides a
cloudy picture. The economy of democratic Japan

has boomed, while many dictators in Africa and Latin America have ruined their economies.

Since citation of examples is unconclusive, it is necessary to consider systematically the relation between economic growth and the political system for many countries. I have related the rates of growth in real per capita gross domestic product since 1950 of almost 60 countries to a few variables, including a measure of the degree of political democracy in each country. These measures, prepared by Raymond Gastil, begin only in 1973, but since the degree of democracy usually changed slowly during the past several decades, they are probably reasonably good estimates in most cases of the degree of democracy during the 1950s and 1960s.

My preliminary results confirm the evidence from several other studies that per capita income growth is positively, not negatively, related to the degree of political democracy. World income grew much more rapidly from 1950 to 1970 than from 1970 to 1985, but the association between growth and democracy is positive and about as strong in the earlier buoyant period as in the later more depressed period.

Although countries with higher per capita income tend to be more democratic, the positive relation between growth and democracy is not due to any beneficial effects of higher income on growth. Democracy appears to increase rates of growth even when the level of per capita income is held constant. It is possible, however, that higher incomes encourage aspirations that propel a country toward greater political democracy.

Apparently, long-term growth is not more erratic under the open and intense competition among interest groups in democracies. Growth in per capita GNP from 1950 to 1985 was no more variable among the democratic than the undemocratic countries.

Political and civil freedoms are so highly

correlated across countries that the variable used
to measure the degree of democracy is also a proxy
for civil liberties. Honest courts, equality
before the law, and other civil liberties are
likely to encourage growth if only because
businessmen and workers investing in physical and
human capital and entering into employment and
other contracts can then count on "due process" in
the resolution of conflicts. Indeed, a few
studies do suggest that civil freedom is more
important than democracy in promoting growth.
Still, nothing in these results or in mine implies
that political democracy is bad for growth.
    Theoretical considerations as well as the
experience of many countries during the past
several decades indicate that democracy broadens
political freedom without retarding economic
growth. This should be reassuring to the several
countries in the midst of converting from
autocratic to democratic systems.

Conclusions

    Adam Smith had the great insight that
selfishness in private transactions works
surprisingly well much of the time to promote
social welfare. When it does not work well,
government intervention could improve matters.
But since political decisions are also dominated
by selfish individuals, actual governments do not
automatically improve rather than worsen the
outcome of private transactions. The major
difficulty in actual political decisions is that
pressure groups use the power of the State to
promote their own interests. A desirable
political system tries to minimize the harm and
maximize the benefits from the political
competition among interest groups.
    The founding fathers of the United States were
well aware of the political power of special
interests:

A landed interest, a manufacturing interest, a
mercantile interest, a monied interest, with
many lesser interests, grow up of necessity in
civilized nations, and divide them into
different classes... The regulation of these
various and interfering interests forms the
principal task of modern legislation, and
involves the spirit of party and faction in the
necessary and ordinary operations of the
government (Hamilton, Jay, and Madison 1941,
56).

The challenging problem for modern societies is to
control the political power of special interests
that advocate policies which lower efficiency and
social output, while at the same time promoting
the power of interest groups, including groups
motivated by selfish considerations, that push for
policies which contribute to efficiency and a
healthy society.

Notes

1. Much of this essay is taken from Becker (1985a, 1985b).
2. See Peltzman's (1988) review of the consistency of the deregulation
movement with these models.

References

Becker, Gary S., "A Theory of Competition Among
    Pressure Groups for Political Influence," The
    Quarterly Journal of Economics 98 (1983):   371-
    400.
_____, "Special Interests and Public Policies,"
    Acceptance Paper, The Frank E. Seidman
    Distinguished Award in Political Economy,
    Rhodes College, September 1985a.
_____, "Public Policies, Pressure Groups, and
    Dead Weight Costs," Journal of Public Economics
    38 (1985b):   329-347.
Brennan, Geoffrey and James M. Buchanan, "The
    Logic of Levers: The Pure Theory of Electoral

Preference." Paper delivered at a conference on the Political Economy of Public Policy, Stanford Center for Public Policy Research 1984.

Carron, Andrew S., "The Political Economy of Financial Regulation," in Roger G. Noll and Bruce M. Owen, eds., The Political Economy of Deregulation, Washington, D.C.: American Enterprise Institute, 1983, 69-83.

Hamilton, Alexander, John Jay, and James Madison, The Federalist, New York: Modern Library, 1941.

Jarrell, Gregg A., "Change at the Exchange: The Causes and Effects of Deregulation," Journal of Law and Economics 27 (1984): 273-312.

Olson, Mancur, Jr., The Rise and Decline of Nations, New Haven: Yale University Press, 1982.

Peltzman, Sam, "The Economic Theory of Regulation in Light of a Decade of Deregulation," University of Chicago. Forthcoming in Brookings Papers on Economic Activity Washington, D.C.: Brookings Institution, 1988.

Smith, Adam, An Inquiry into the Nature and Causes of the Wealth of Nations, New York: Modern Library 1937.

_____, The Theory of Moral Sentiments, E. G. West, ed., New Rochelle: Arlington House, 1968.

Spiller, Pablo T., "The Differential Impact of Airline Regulation on Individual Firms and Markets: An Empirical Analysis," Journal of Law and Economics 26 (1983): 655-689.

3

BOOTLEGGERS AND BAPTISTS IN THE MARKET FOR REGULATION
Bruce Yandle

In the Beginning

Regulation of individual behavior by higher authorities is as ancient as the Garden of Eden and as recent as yesterday's <u>Federal Register</u>. Adam and Eve chaffed against the iron-clad specification standard they confronted, accepted the advice of an independent counselor, engaged in noncompliance activities, and suffered the consequences. They were required to leave a pristine environment where entry was barred and move to a significantly deteriorated competitive location where labor productivity was lower and future regulations would be crafted by their fellow man.

Still today, many people are frustrated by complex environmental rules, seek wise counsel as to how to deal with them, and sometimes pay high penalties when they fail to satisfy the regulator. On the other hand, other people complain about the lack of rules, seek more of them, and lobby fiercely for stricter enforcement.

Yet a third group of people from within the ranks of the frustrated and penalized silently accept regulation and welcome the support of those who seek more of it. Indeed, a careful

examination of most any successful regulatory
episode suggests that there are winners and losers
at the margin, but also that the hats worn by the
participants are rarely all black or all white.
We understand that regulation, like taxation,
redistributes wealth and carries costs. We also
know that regulatory reform, like tax reform,
alters the former redistribution effects and may
relieve some of the burdens of regulation,
provided the key parties that originally sought
the regulation somehow support the changes.

What Theory Tells Us

The economic literature on regulation and
efforts by special interest groups to gain favors
from government--whether they be members of the
steel industry or the Sierra Club--illuminates
some of the dimensions of the demand for
regulation, at least for some of the people in a
regulation story. We now understand that some
regulated firms view regulation favorably, once
they realize government intervention is
inevitable. Regulation is not necessarily a
government-designed hair shirt that constantly
limits the desired actions of these firms. It is
more like an old tweed suit that not only fits but
also feels good. Indeed, those in the tweed suits
get upset when efficiency lovers suggest that the
government-imposed suit should be thrown away.
They do not want deregulation. Regulation has
tilted the economic game in their direction and
now protects their position.
Their long-suffering compatriots, scratching in
their hair shirts, feel differently about the
matter, but may not be very successful in a
showdown, because they lack the support of another
group: Those who seek regulation for reasons that
have nothing to do with anti-competitive tweed
suits. In other words, there are coalitions that
work and others that do not.

The modern theories of regulation that carry us
beyond the noble public interest story gain
considerable yardage in explaining important
aspects of many regulations. A widely cited
theory of regulation developed by Richard Posner
causes us to focus on transfers of wealth from
politically weak to stronger groups.[1] Fundamental
work by Nobel Laurette George Stigler and Sam
Peltzman ask us to consider special interest
groups, to look for differential effects across
those groups, and to view regulation as a market
process with demanders and suppliers.[2] Stigler
and Peltzman also argue that most successful
regulation will generate some benefits to
consumers, even though the favored producer group
will likely gain the most. Gordon Tullock and
Nobel Laurette James Buchanan, who are the
founders of the Public Choice school in economics
and political science, call our attention to rent-
seeking behavior, where government's power to
limit competition and output always beckon and
where seekers of government favors tend to spend
the value of their expected gains while chasing
them.[3] Tullock and Buchanan observe regulation as
a way to restrict output, raise price, and
foreclose markets to new competition.
     Fred McChesney notes that politicians can act
as agents in the regulatory game, profiting
regardless of the result.[4] He suggests that
politicians can propose harsh rules that cause the
affected individuals to organize politically and
lobby for relief, which strengthens the
politician's position. Once the rules are in
place, the organized group will continue to lobby,
supporting those politicians who are sympathetic
to their cause. Gary Becker directs our
attention to coalitions that favor and oppose
actions by government to redistribute wealth,
whether that is done by taxing and spending or by
rent-generating regulations that impose a tax to
be shared by one and all in the form of deadweight

cost to the economy.[5] His analysis focuses on
political actions and reactions that are induced
when groups seeking governmental favors are
countered by others who bear the net cost of those
actions.

A Neglected Point

A host of empirical work now lends strong
support to elements of each of these compatible
theories. However, while there is room in the new
theories for a neglected focus, none of the
theories emphasizes the potential importance of
having public interest support for successful
regulatory ventures. It is as though the public
interest theory--the pure notion that political
agents are dedicated to serving a collective
public interest--died from over-exposure to better
theories and left no heirs. I argue that
politicians in a democracy must find ways to dress
their actions in public interest clothing. Highly
visible special interest benefits just cannot be
transferred in the raw.

To make the point, consider these questions.
Would the Act to Regulate Commerce that produced
the Interstate Commerce Commission in 1887 have
passed without the support of Populists who
thought they were getting the best of the
railroads? Would the English Factory Acts that
arguably gave an advantage to capital intensive
firms have been passed without the movement
against child labor? Would federal meat
inspection and the associated limits on the
importation of foreign beef have made it on the
law books without stories of poison food and an
associated public outcry? I say "No" to these
questions. But saying no is not enough. We need
to know more about how a "moral majority" becomes
valuable in the political economy of regulation.
Think about coalitions of groups that support
government action where the coalition includes

some that seek directly enhanced wealth and others that wish for an improved vision of society.

This chapter focuses on that particular coalition of interest groups that always seems present in a successful regulatory episode. The chapter addresses economic and social regulation, the rules that dictate methods of production and consumption, where the focus is on functions within firms and those that affect industry behavior with respect to price and entry.[6] The chapter presents a theory of durable regulation-- the theory of Bootleggers and Baptists--and provides summaries of regulatory events that appear to be explained by the theory.

The Theory of Bootleggers and Baptists

Bootleggers and Baptists have historically supported a form of social regulation that closes corner liquor stores on Sunday. The two groups are very distinctive, even though we can refer to their joint effort as forming a coalition. Think about their differences. Bootleggers are generally not accepted in polite Baptist company, certainly not when wearing tags that identify their occupations. Of course, some bootleggers may be Baptist, but the brethren don't advertise that in the Sunday bulletin. Now, consider their common interest--Sunday closing laws that shut down the corner liquor stores. The bootleggers want to eliminate direct competition. The Baptists want to reduce indirect competition and diminish the consumption of alcoholic bevereges.

But when we say they both lobby, we must add quickly that the lobbying occurs in markedly different ways. The bootleggers do not organize walks, parades, letter writing campaigns or sit- ins at state capital buildings. They confront the politicians more furtively, yet more positively. The Baptists bring something to the anti- competitive effort that cannot be delivered by bootleggers. They add public interest content to what otherwise would be a strictly private venture. The Baptist element, which I ask you to think of as a generic term, adds a moral ring to what might otherwise be viewed as an immoral effort, the passing of money (and electability) to politicians to obtain a political favor.

Probing deeper into this notion, think about the design of the regulation delivered to bootleggers and Baptists. The common regulation does not consist of higher taxes on alcohol, that is, the use of economic incentives, even though efficiency-driven economists might term that approach the more efficient one. Nor does it address the Sunday consumption or possession of alcolohic beverages. It is command and control regulation that focuses solely on the sale of the product. If a diminution in the consumption of the liquid were the over-riding goal, a public interest theory would likely predict consumption to be the offense. Going further, a pure public interest argument might conclude that higher taxes on the undesired beverages would address the problem. Of course, monitoring and enforcement costs have to be considered. There is, after all, a supply side to all regulatory problems. But as Becker reminds us, the wealth-redistributing regulation obtained is probably the most efficient in that set; which is to say that both the bootleggers and the Baptists have to be satisfied with the final equilibrium.

Interestingly, regulations of the Sunday sale of booze tie together bootleggers, Baptists, and the legal operators of liquor stores. The bootleggers buy from the legal outlets on Saturday, sell at higher prices on Sunday, and the Baptists praise the effort to enforce the regulatory cartel. Meanwhile, the political suppliers of the regulation reap the support of all the groups, and the Internal Revenue Service

works to prevent market entry by those who would
produce alcoholic beverages on homemade stills.

What might cause the coalition to crumble, so
that we might observe the repeal of Sunday closing
laws? To answer that question, we must consider
some elements of regulatory demand. First, the
Baptist appeal works so long as most of the
Baptists recognize and accept the over-riding
moral argument, so long as the group continues to
represent a politically valuable interest group,
and so long as group leaders are able to marshall
resources from the members. There is always a
potential free rider problem in such ventures.
What we term the public interest is defined by
public opinion, but delivering political support
is fraught with practical problems.

Next, the bootleggers must earn a high enough
return from their endeavor to buy political
favors. If entry occurs in their market--by means
of more illicit stills, lower cost transportation
from locations that have no restrictions, or by
the expansion of lower cost private clubs that
offer the restricted beverage to their members, or
if demand for the product simply diminishes, the
bootleggers will be pushed from the picture. Once
the restriction either ceases to be binding or
loses its moral support, we predict regulatory
reform and the possible replacement of bootleggers
by another politically powerful interest group,
such as the private club owners.

While bootleggers and Baptists are dominant
figures in the theory, there are always other
groups who bear the costs of the restriction.
They too can become more powerful, especially as
the costs of the restriction rise, and exert
enough force to overcome the political demands of
the dominant group. Opportunity cost tends always
to raise its head.

An examination of several recent regulatory
episodes will illustrate some of these analytical
points. To give a flavor of some research and

findings, four regulatory stories can be
considered: State regulations of Sunday retail
sales, or Blue Laws; federal regulation of
flammable sleepwear; state regulation of gambling,
or lottery laws; and a state/federal episode
involving seatbelts and airbags.

State Blue Laws

State Blue Laws are kissing cousins of Sunday
Closing Laws that make a market for bootleggers.[7]
Both regulations date back to colonial times,
probably reflecting religious preferences of the
time. Indeed, the term "Blue Law" takes its name
from the color of the paper on which early
colonial statutes were written. The modern period
finds Blue Laws in a gradual state of decline.
For example, in 1970, 25 states had restrictive
statutes. By 1984, only 14 states remained in the
fold, and others were threatening to modify or
repeal outright the remaining vestiges of the
centuries-old institution. The systematic
disappearance of Blue Laws provides an opportunity
for researchers to examine the shifting support
for the law and so to identify what might motivate
the political economy that delivers the rules.

Research on this topic focused on theoretical
notions about the demand for Blue Laws and from
that developed statistical models that might test
the theory. To capture changes in Blue Laws, data
for 1970 and 1984 were examined. The theoretical
arguments played on the theme of bootleggers and
Baptists. We argued that Blue Laws preserve
retailers' revenues while distributing those
revenues over fewer operating hours and increasing
the average per customer purchase. Since their
organizing costs are already covered, we argued
that unions might be better positioned to bargain
for higher wages, though we recognized that most
retail establishments are not unionized. We also
argued that unionized labor forces have more
predictable and uniform work hours and holidays,

which means restrictions on Sunday shopping carry
lower opportunity costs for unionized communities.
Union workers were first members of the bootlegger
group that might favor Blue Laws.

We then thought about bootleggers on the side
of repealing Blue Laws. Among various retailers,
we predicted large drug stores would fight Sunday
restrictions, since they must operate their core
businesses on Sunday, have variable costs covered,
but are limited by Blue Laws in selling a portion
of their inventories defined as "nonessential."
On the other hand, we predicted large general
retailers would support the laws in the pre-mall
1970 period, since those establishments were
geared to compete for downtown shoppers who
wouldn't likely flock to the cities on Sundays.
In the later period, we predicted large retailers
would be either indifferent or opposed to Blue
Laws. The large stores might be termed
backsliding bootleggers.

The opportunity cost of shopping entered our
analysis in another way. Historically, women have
specialized in shopping. As the average workers'
real wage fell, more women entered the work force,
the opportunity cost of Blue Laws rose. The
percent of women in the labor force proxied for
neither bootleggers or Baptists, but simply served
in our research as an indicator of the cost of the
restriction. However, in the earlier period of
the analysis, we argued that the widely fractured
population of women workers faced a high cost of
organizing politically. Later, and due to other
causes, women became a more identifiable interest
group.

The chief Baptist element in our analysis was
the Baptists themselves. We used the percent of
the population Southern Baptist, an organized
interest group that polices free riding with
sanctions delivered by conventions, as a proxy for
a moral majority that favored Sunday restrictions.

The statistical counterpart of our theory used a "yes, a state has Blue Laws/no, it does not" indicator as the dependent variable and included the arguments mentioned as independent variables. Our statistical findings, which are reported in Table 3-1, indicate that the share Baptist has a strong positive association with Blue Laws in 1970, but none in 1984. The Baptist effect seemed to dissipate over time. The percent union is not significant in either period. However, the number of retail stores with more than 100 employees is positively associated with Blue Law status in the 1970 pre-shopping mall period, but has no association in 1984, when larger retail stores were generally found in suburban shopping centers. Drug stores are negatively associated with Blue Laws in 1970, but not associated in 1984.

Briefly stated, we found support for both parts of the theory. Large retail stores and women appear to be bootleggers in the early period. Indeed, work opportunities for women in the early period were associate largely with downtown retail stores and offices. We speculate that having a Sunday holiday appears to have been more important than having opportunities to shop on Sunday. Drug stores bore a cost in the early period, and Baptists played the expected Baptist role. As time passed and the nature of female employment changed, women apparently bore more of the regulation's cost. The Baptist influence, which may have been delivered in large part by women, eroded, and all other significant opposition faded. Blue Laws were repealed.

Table 3-1.   Regression Results. Dependent Variable:
Blue Law Indicator

Variable	1970		1984	
	1	2	1	2
Intercept	2.414 (0.871)[a]	2.535 (0.979)	0.1204 (0.095)	0.3487 (0.436)
Date	-0.001 (1.178		-0.0004 (0.295)	
Bapt.	0.0325 (3.291)	0.0317 (4.271)	0.0090 (0.503)	
Party	-0.0018 (0.285)		-0.0019 (1.995)	0.0156 (3.767)
Union	0.0092 (1.015)	0.0115 (1.388)	0.0063 (0.662)	
Women	0.0168 (2.762)	0.0185 (3.311)	-0.0243 (1.535)	
SML	-0.00004 (1.501)	-0.0004 (1.688)	-0.0001 (0.864)	
Large	0.0038 (2.712)	0.0026 (2.673)	0.0005 (0.671)	
Drug	-0.0053 (2.595)	-0.0051 (2.581)	0.0004 (0.264)	
Tour	-0.0006 (0.831)		-0.00006 (0.662)	
R^2	.37	.38	.20	.27
F	4.20	5.47	2.37	10.24

[a]Absolute value of t-statistics in parentheses.

Note: Variables in model, not mentioned in text include: Party:
The share of legislative seats controlled by the majority state
party and TOUR: which is annual dollars of tourism spending.

Flame Resistant Sleepwear

An episode involving the Consumer Product Safey
Commission's (CPSC's) 1971 imposition of a
flammability regulation for children's sleepwear
is particularly interesting, since the agency
later, in 1977, banned the chief chemical agent
used by industry for meeting the flammability
regulation.[8] The chemical, Tris, was found to be
a carcinogen.   We learned from an examination
of background data that Asian-produced sleepwear
had taken a substantial part of the U.S., U.K,
Canadian, and European markets prior to the CPSC
regulation. The U.S. and U.K. adopted
flammability standards at the same time, and
foreign penetration of their markets fell
markedly. That did not occur in the other
developed markets that had no flammability
standards. We were suspicious.

In this research, we argued that domestic
sleepwear producers gained increased market share
from the flammability regulation, but did not
likely gain much in the way of profits. Entry is
relatively quick and easy in that end of the
apparel industry. Thinking more about industry
supply curves, we argued that certain producers of
synthetic fibers gained from the rules, since
cotton fiber and fabric could not meet the CPSC
standard. Cotton's market share fell to zero
after the regulation. Finally, we argued that the
producers of Tris, the chemical selected to meet
the standard by virtually all in the yarn and
fabric industry, gained from the standard. The
product was patented, and five U.S. firms were
licensed to produce and market it. They had the
most inelastic supply curve of all. Focusing on
the demand side, we argued that the demand for the
flammability treatment was very inelastic, since
it was mandated by law and there were few if any
substitutes. That made the burden of the
restriction quite palatable.

Although we contend that cotton producers bore

the brunt of the industry cost in the episode, we
argued they were guarded from losses by a long-
standing government-sponsored cartel. The U.S.
Department of Agriculture protects cotton
producers through acreage and price controls.
Perhaps that is partly why a rule destroying a
small market for cotton goods could make it
through the political thicket.

Using an import penetration model and then
financial markets analysis of portfolios of
apparel, fabric, fiber, and chemical firms, we
tested for effects. The results of the import
penetration model, reported in Table 3-2, provided
strong support for the theory that import
penetration fell markedly with the imposition of
the flammability rule. We also found strong
support for the notion of financial gains for
fiber and Tris producers. But we found no
evidence of gains for apparel and fabric
producers, while recognizing that most of the
apparel firms were too small to be accounted for
in our financial markets tests.

This research suggests the bootleggers were the
owners of specialized capital in the chemical and
fiber industries. But who were the Baptists?
They were the parents of children, and other
consumer groups, who pressured the CPSC to develop
an all-encompassing flammability standard, a rule
that would spread the cost of a desired feature
across all consumers in the market. Along these
lines, a 1971 report in Chemical and Engineering
News stated: "An unlikely coalition of mothers
and some chemical companies is pleased with the
newly promulgated standard."[9] By our theory, the
coalition was not an unlikely one.

Of course, the ban on Tris unraveled all this.
Unfortunately, the CPSC rule had the effect of
spreading a cancer risk across an entire
population of young children. There was an

Table 3-2.   Regression Results. Dependent Variable:
              Imported Sleepwear/Domestic Sleepwear

Variable	Coefficient	T-Statistic
Intercept	-0.1970	-0.565
Income	1.2248E-07	3.148
Price	-0.3783	-2.129
Dum 72	-0.2117	-4.847
Dum 75	-0.0760	-2.093
Ban	-0.3482	-4.688

R^2 :   .68

F   :   8.30

Durbin-Watson: 1.825

Note: The independent variables adjust for real total disposable
INCOME, the ratio fo the domestic apparel PRICE index to the all
item CPI, the July 1972 flammability regulation--DUM 72, a 1975
regulation that expanded coverage of the previous rule--DUM 75,
and the later BAN on chemically treated sleepwear that came in
1977.

understandable public outcry to the news about
Tris. The ban that ended that part of the episode
resulted in large financial losses for the
chemical industry and smaller ones for the fiber
industry. The Tris episode was a case of
regulatory failure for all parties, except
possibly the political agents who managed it.
    The ending of the story illustrates another
point: When the bootleggers lose the Baptists,
the regulation goes away.

State Regulation of Gambling
    Government sponsored gambling can be traced

back at least as far as Caesar Augustus, who
instituted lotteries for the purpose of rebuilding
Rome. They were used by Queen Elizabeth to help
fund the Virginia Company's founding of Jamestown.
But in more recent times, state-operated lotteries
have emerged as a durable source of revenues for
state governments.[10]
     On its face, gambling is a moral issue to many
religious groups. And proposals to institute
state lotteries are always opposed by
denominational groups. The Baptist element that
opposes this state regulation is apparent. That
being so, why have lotteries become so popular in
recent years? Is this a case like Blue Laws,
where moral influence seems to have been swamped
by other effects? At present, 28 states have
lotteries, up from one in 1964, and their net
proceeds in 1986 amounted to more than $5 billion.
     Our research on this topic sought to explain
state intervention to operate lotteries across
states in the face of moral opposition. In our
theory, we argued that marginal analyses were made
during each legislative session, which is to say
that laws could be passed or repealed each year.
We first noted that when lottery revenues are
viewed as tax revenues they are highly regressive.
Put differently, state-operated lotteries provide
an opportunity to transfer income from lower-to
higher-income taxpayers, which gives the first
bootlegger clue.
     We also observed that the ever-present demand
for gambling, which is relatively inelastic, can
be satisfied by either private or public means,
and that private provision occurs legally and
illegally. If states are to enter the market
successfully, they must find ways to limit their
competition. That led us to say that states
operating a monopoly lottery will generally have a
larger police operation than other states, all
else equal.
     In the analysis, the demand for repeal, as

observed in the nonlottery states, was driven by
the Baptist element, which we proxied by the
percent of the population holding that faith.
Demand for lotteries was driven by higher income
people, proxied by average per capita income, with
stronger support coming where state debt per
capita was higher and where states had a
constitutional requirement for a balanced budget.
The number of police, weighted by population,
entered the analysis to determine its relationship
with lottery status. We also included state taxes
per capita in our model that explained the
occurence of lotteries, suggesting that taxes were
a substitute for lotteries. The higher those
taxes, the less likely a lottery would exist, all
else equal.

Focusing on current data in our statistical
testing, our estimate, reported in Table 3-3,
found the percent Baptist to be negatively
associated with lotteries, debt per capita and
income per capita positively related, and police
per capita positively related. The presence of a
balanced budget requirement was not quite
significant, though its sign was positive. We
also found state taxes per capita negatively
associated with lotteries, which supports the
notion that lotteries are a substitute for taxes.

This analysis suggests how other forces can
overwhelm a moral element. That is, the
bootleggers overwhelmed the Baptists. But we
cannot say that Baptists are no longer
influential. A related question remains to be
resolved. Most states that pass lotteries earmark
the funds for some popular social purpose--such as
for education. Quite possibly, the bootleggers
gain the support of the Baptists by providing an
apparent link to a public interest cause that
offsets the gambling stigma.

Table 3-3.   Regression Results. Dependent Variable:
            Lottery States (Yes = 1; No = 0)

Variable	Coefficient	T-Statistic
Intercept	0.3582	0.758
Income	0.854	2.212
Police	0.572	1.676
Debt	0.1584	2.046
Tax	-0.1028	3.376
Balance	0.2738	1.382
Baptist	-0.0254	4.393
R^2 : 47		
F : 8.36		

Note: Independent variables are: Per capita state INCOME,
Number of POLICE per 1000 population, State DEBT per capita,
Occurence of constitutional BALANCE budget requirement (yes=1,
no=0), Percent of state population that is Southern BAPTIST.

Federally Mandated Air Bags

A last regulatory episode dealt with a very
complicated effort by the federal government to
mandate the installation of passive restraints in
automobiles.[11] The episode began officially in
1969 with an Advance Notice of Proposed Rulemaking
issued by the National Highway Safety
Administration (NHTSA), followed by a 1971 final
rule and a mass of actions, reactions and delays
of implementation; and ending with a 1984
Department of Transportation action requiring

states to settle the issue by voting. After two decades, this regulatory issue is still unresolved.

Air bags became a meaningful topic of conversation in the late 1960s when a bulge of people entering the 16-25 age group contributed to a significant increase in auto fatalities. Of course, that was the period when multiple forces contributed to the development of a regulatory binge in Washington, with many new agencies being formed, additional laws passed, and thousands of new regulations placed on the books.

The air bag had been used in to protect test pilots in the development of aircraft, and one of the bag manufacturers approached NHTSA about requiring that the device be used in all new automobiles. They believed that air bags would protect drivers who chose not to use seat belts.

Interest in air bags increased, and Ford Motor Company joined Eaton Manufacturing Company to demonstrate the first working air bag at an engineering society meeting in early 1968. Soon thereafter, Ford became discouraged about the bag's prospects, noting serious problems for out-of-position passenger's and the probability that passengers would be seriously injured by inflating bags. It was also clear that seat belts still would be needed in combination with bags to meet the rules NHTSA was contemplating.   General Motors then became the leading proponent for air bags and demonstrated its ability to build bag-equipped autos early on. With that, NHTSA proposed its passive restraint rule, and GM indicated it would strive to meet the standard with air bags. The other major auto producers sued NHTSA. Eventually much more was learned about air bags, auto safety, and the consumers' willingness to buy bag-equipped cars. Along the way, Sam Peltzman shook the cage of safety scholars with his finding that cars equipped with safety equipment could induce a lulling effect

that caused drivers to sustain more instead of
fewer injuries.[12] That did not slow the
regulatory juggernaut, but other political and
market events did.

Who were the supporters of air bags?
Obviously, the holders of air bag patents. But
the auto insurance industry was the strongest and
most persistent advocate of all. Why might this
be so? Surely, other groups interested in safety
and health would be counted first.

Auto insurers can gain from passive restraints
in several ways. First, the insurers could
determine risk easier where passive restraints are
used. Unlike belts, the mere presence of bags
insures protection to the head and upper body in
the event of a head-on accident.   Second, they
could earn one-time gains from contracts written
on the basis of higher risks, which would be
reduced by the installation of passive restraints.
Third, a reduction in head-related injuries--the
most expensive of all--would reduce the cost of
extensive injury-related litigation, which would
reduce price and expand markets. In addition to
these reasons for supporting the regulation, as a
regulated industry, insurance firms could gain
demand for their product by means of the publicity
accompanying a long and controversial regulatory
proceeding and encounter little competitive
response in doing so. Along with the insurance
firms, General Motors was a potential winner, at
least in the beginning of the episode. Its
competition was behind in developing bag-equipped
cars. A rule requiring bags would raise
competitors' costs.

Who were the Baptists? All those who responded
to the promise of safer cars and reduced
fatalities. As some might put it, how could
anyone be opposed to auto safety? Ralph Nader's
Center for Auto Safey, funded largely by the auto
insurance industry, was chief among the
organizations that prompted this support.

Financial markets analysis was used to estimate abnormal returns for portfolios of auto manufacturers, air bag manufacturers, and insurance firms. The analytical approach forms a portfolio of the relevant stocks and compares its performance to the entire New York Stock Exchange's performance in association with specific events. Sudden changes in the returns to the portfolio relative to the exchange are then identified. In all, 10 key events that might have increased or decreased the wealth of the portfolio shareholders as the rules were imposed, delayed, modified, and finally put to state vote. While there were mixed results for a number of the events, we observed that air bag producers gained substantial wealth when the passive restraint rule was introduced. Ford and Chrysler suffered cumulative losses, but neither GM nor AMC suffered a loss in association with the initial rule.

When NHTSA delayed the rule in 1970, both the insurance industry and air bag portfolios sustained abnormal losses. However, the delay did not generate gains for the auto portfolio, partly because the delay was accompanied by additional safety standards that related to padding and interior design. In yet another event, in 1980 when Congress passed legislation delaying the standard again but requiring passive restraints to be met by producers of smaller cars first--a barrier to the flood of imported cars, both the automakers and air bag producers experienced abnormal gains.

In other work, we examined the later state votes on mandatory seat belts, which could result in the elimination of passive restraint requirements. A vote for mandatory belts was a vote against mandatory passive restraints. Our estimating equation for explaining whether or not a mandatory seat belt referendum was passed, used 1986 data, and the results are reported in Table 3-4. As indicated there, we found that the number

of auto frames produced in a state was positively
associated with passage. By the time of the vote,
auto producers were generally opposed to passive
restraints. Earlier efforts to market bags had
not been successful and the required installation
of passive restraints in smaller cars would
significantly raise price. The presence of an air
bag manufacturer in a state had strong negative
partial effects, and the number of employees in a
state's fire, marine, and casualty insurance
sector, weighted by population, was negatively
associated with passage of mandatory seat belt
laws. They wanted passive restraints.

Table 3-4.   Regression Results. Dependent Variable:
             State Passage of Mandatory Belt Law (Yes = 1; No = 0)

Variable	Coefficient	T-Statistic
Intercept	−1.4184	−2.621
Auto	0.24 E-6	2.098
Insur	−0.1814	−2.428
Air	−0.5453	−2.343
Phys	0.0021	1.001
NOF	−0.1914	−1.646
Educ	0.0280	3.190
High	−22.104	−3.756
Inc	0.00005	1.150

R^2 : .50

Durbin-Watson: 1.92

Note: Independent variables are: Total number of AUTO
assemblies produced annually in each state; the total number of
workers in the insurance industry weighted by population for each
state, an AIRbag dummy variable (yes=1, no=0) for states with an
airbag producer; number of PHYSICIANS per 100,000 people, a dummy
variable for no-fault insurance states, NOF; the percentage
population having received a high school diploma; and per capita
INCOME by state.

In terms of bootleggers and Baptists, the passive restraint research suggests that auto insurance companies, the producers of air bags, and at one point, the leading auto producer were early bootleggers. Public interest groups took the moral high ground and gained financial support from some bootleggers. As time passed, and import penetration increased, a carefully molded passive restraint rule was seen as a way to restrain to competition. The ranks of the bootleggers increased and moved in lock step with the Baptists. Eventually, belts and bags competed in a political economy with bootleggers and Baptists. Meanwhile, technology advanced, prices of passive restraints fell, and more producers began to offer the item as standard equipment in higher priced cars.

Concluding Thoughts

The theory of Bootleggers and Baptists argues that ideology matters in the political economy of regulation, but it matters in a very specific way. When considering the effective demand for regulation and the final form taken by specific rules, we must look for an important group of demanders who deliver public interest content to the regulatory cause. In the first place, there is considerable competition for political favors, and a politician must be able to explain his actions. That being so, we should expect to find strong public interest statements about the virtues of regulation that can be ratified by important social groups and figures. We should recognize that groups like the Environmental Defense Fund and the Sierra Club, just to name two, are vital to the passage of clean air legislation. We should also recognize that the support of those groups can be quite valuable to polluters who seek a particular form of regulation, a form that may raise their competitor's costs or in other ways improve the future profits of an industry group.

The struggle for regulation that best serves the bootlegger-Baptist coalition occurs at the federal level. It is difficult to gain very much in a competitive environment across 50 states. In a similar way, the outcomes predicted for the theory seldom apply to actions taken by courts. The theory best explains legislative and regulatory actions where the political process can be affected through lobbying, campaign contributions, and efforts by politicians to satisfy constituent groups.

The evolution of environmental regulation in the U.S. allows us to observe just how much a special interest theory of regulation might explain. In the chapters to follow, direct references will be made to interest groups struggles, but while it may be apparent from the stories, members of the groups will never be referred to directly as "bootleggers" or "Baptists."

Notes

1. See Posner (1974).
2. See Peltzman (1976) and Stigler (1971).
3. See Tullock (1967) and Buchanan (1980).
4. See McChesney (1987).
5. See Becker (1983).
6. See Yandle and Young (1986).
7. This discussion is drawn from Price and Yandle (1987).
8. This section is drawn from Shuford and Yandle (1988).
9. See "Flammability Rule Argued," Chemical and Engineering News, April 9, 1971, 9.
10. This section is based on Martin and Yandle (1988).
11. This section is based on Kneuper (1987).
12. See Peltzman (1975). For more on this see Crandall (1986).

References

Anderson, Douglas D. Regulatory Politics and Electric Utilities. Boston: Auburn House Publishing, 1981.

Becker, Gary S. "A Theory of Competition Among Pressure Groups for Political Influence." The Quarterly Journal of Economics 98(August 1983): 371-399.

Buchanan, James M. "Rent Seeking and Profit Seeking." in Toward a Theory of the Rent-Seeking Society, ed. by J. M. Buchanan, R. D. Tollison, and G. Tulluck, College Station: Texas A&M Press, 1980.

Crandall, Robert. Regulating the Automobile, Washington: Brookings Institution, 1986.

"Flammability Rules Argued." Chemical and Engineering News (April 1971).

Irwin, Manley R. "The Telephone Industry." Walter Adams, ed. The Structure of American Industry. New York: Macmillan Publishing Company, 1982, 298-318.

Kneuper, Robert A. "The Political Economy of Mandatory Passive Restraints: An Investigation of Auto Safety Regulation." Master's thesis, Department of Economics, Clemson University, 1987.

Martin, Robert and Bruce Yandle. "Lotteries as Transfer Mechanisms." Unpublished manuscript, Department of Economics, Clemson University, 1988.

McChesney, Fred S. "Rent Extraction and Rent Creation in the Economic Theory of Regulation." The Journal of Legal Studies 16(1987): 101-117.

Peltzman, Sam. "The Effects of Automobile Safety Regulation." Journal of Political Economy. 83(Aug.-Dec. 1975): 677-725.

_____. "Toward a More General Theory of Regulation." Journal of Law and Economics. 19(August 1976): 211-240.

Posner, Richard A. "Theories of Economic Regulation." Bell Journal 5(Autumn 1974): 335-358.

Price, Jamie and Bruce Yandle. "Labor Markets and Sunday Closing Laws." Journal of Labor Research

8(Fall 1987): 407-413.
Shuford, Gordon and Bruce Yandle. "Consumer
Protection, Private Interests Effects, and
Government Liability: The Tris Episode."
Center for Policy Studies, Clemson University,
1988.
Stiger, George J. "The Theory of Economic
Regulation." Bell Journal of Economics 2(Spring
1971): 3-21.
Tullock, Gordon. "The Welfare Costs of Tariffs,
Monopolies, and Theft." Western Economic
Journal 5(June 1967): 224-232.
Yandle, Bruce. "Bootleggers and Baptists: The
Education of a Regulatory Economist."
Regulation (May/June 1983): 12-16.
_____. "Intertwined Interests, Rent Seeking and
Regulation." Social Science Quarterly
65(December 1984): 1004-1012.
_____ and Elizabeth Young. "Regulating the
Function, Not the Industry." Public Choice
51(1986): 56-69.

4

PARTIAL REGULATION OF NATURAL MONOPOLY
John Tschirhart

Introduction[1]

A substantial body of economic research over
the past decade or so has been directed at the
regulation of natural monopolies. Indeed the very
definition of natural monopoly has been updated.
Baumol (1977) equated natural monopoly with a firm
whose cost function is subadditive over the
relevant region of production. He then developed
cost concepts for multi-product firms that allow a
better understanding of the conditions that give
rise to natural monopoly. Panzar and Willig
(1977) studied the sustainability of a firm; that
is, can a firm charge prices for its outputs that
will thwart competitive entry. And Baumol, Panzar
and Willig (1982) introduced contestability, a
measure of the ease with which new firms can enter
an industry. The work of these authors and
others has led to a reevaluation of the market and
technological conditions that justify when a
natural monopoly should or should not be
regulated.[2]

But while economists were leaping toward
improved regulatory policies, they were being
leap-frogged by policy makers. In the past decade
there have been sweeping and profound changes in
regulated industries. The trucking, railroad,

airline, banking, electricity, telecommunications
and natural gas industries have all undergone
change. At one extreme is the total deregulation
of price and entry restrictions for airlines on
domestic routes, and at the other extreme is the
modest deregulation of electricity generation
which is in the experimental stage. These changes
have been justified by arguing either that firms
in these industries are not natural monopolies,
that the markets are contestable, or that
technology will be spurred better by competition.
Unfortunately, the evidence supporting these
arguments is seldom clear. And what we now have
are formerly regulated industries that have become
partially regulated, and what we do not have are
useful policy guidelines on how to deal with these
situations.

Partial regulation can come about in several
ways. Multiproduct firms that were previously
constrained by price and entry regulations in all
of their markets may have these constraints lifted
in a subset of their markets, or may have some of
the constraints lifted in all their markets. For
example, manufacturing of terminal equipment for
telecommunications has been completely
deregulated, and greater pricing flexibility is
now available throughout the trucking industry.
Alternatively, firms may still have all of their
old markets subject to price and entry
constraints, but they may be allowed to divest
into new, competitive markets. This occurs in the
telecommunications industry as Judge Greene
permits the Bell Operating Companies to enter
markets where their bottleneck facilities will not
give them a decided advantage.

Pricing and Entry Issues Under Partial Regulation

To introduce the nature of price and entry
issues that arise when firms are partially
regulated, consider a two-product example. In the

example, a comparison will be made between two cases: 1) the two products are produced by two monopolies, each specializing in one product; and 2) the two products are produced by a single, two-product monopoly.   Figure 4-1 displays profit contours in price space for two single-product monopoly firms and for one two-product monopoly firm.   For the case of two single-product monopoly firms, firm i, i=1, 2, earns profit labelled π^i by charging price p^i.   A portion of each firm's zero-profit contour is displayed and labelled accordingly, while inside the contour a firm earns positive profit.   In order for both firms to operate, the price vector $p = (p_1, p_2)$ must fall in area fghk where both firms earn nonnegative profit.   Outside this area, at least one firm earns negative profit.   Profit of each firm is dependent on the other's price, because the products are assumed to be weak gross substitutes in demand.[3]

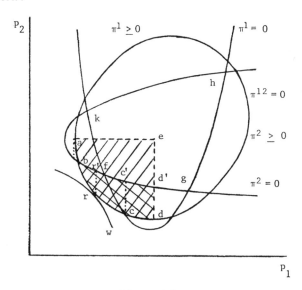

Figure 4-1

As an alternative to two single-product firms, one two-product monopoly firm can produce both products and realize profit π[12]. The complete zero-profit contour is displayed for the two-product firm. Inside the contour, profit is positive and maximum profit is attained at point e.

Figure 4-1 is the type of diagram used by Panzar and Willig (1977) to examine sustainability issues. The Figure shows a sustainable, two-product natural monopoly.[4] Sustainability requires that the monopolist earn zero profit and charge undominated prices,[5] and these conditions are satisfied along arc ad. In addition, sustainability requires that there be no cross subsidies, which narrows the eligible prices to those along arc bc. Neither firm specializing in only one product can earn positive profit by undercutting either of the monopolist's prices if they are along arc bc.[6]

Consider next the following three scenarios. First, suppose a monopolist produces both products in noncontestable markets; that is, there are barriers to entry into both markets perhaps due to sunk costs. Without regulation the monopolist, using undominated prices, can opt for any price vector in the cross-hatched and hatched areas with point e being the preferred price vector. According to the standard policy prescriptions, the welfare oriented regulator's task in this situation is to dictate prices that maximize a welfare criteria (say consumers plus producers surplus) subject to a break even constraint on profit. Given the welfare contour w in Figure 4-1, the dictated prices are given by point r. This point represents the Ramsey prices, which are sustainable in this example. (In general there is no guarantee that Ramsey prices are sustainable: point r need not lie on arc bc.)

In the second scenario, suppose entry barriers are removed and both markets are perfectly

contestable. In order to thwart entry, the
monopolist is compelled by market forces to price
along bc. Moreover, the monopolist may even
choose point r owing to information problems (See
Baumol, Bailey, and Willig 1977). At any rate, in
either scenario one or two, which are referred to
as the totally regulated and the totally
unregulated cases, respectively, either an optimum
regulatory policy or market forces result in a
price vector along bc.

In the third scenario, suppose market two is
contestable and market one is not. Further, the
regulator eschews all price and entry regulation
in the second market; that is, market two is
deregulated relative to scenario one. This
becomes a case of partial regulation. Again
using undominated prices, the monopolist is free
to choose among price vectors in the cross-hatched
area only. But now there are neither market
forces nor regulatory policies to move the
monopolist to bc. Market forces are not present
provided the monopolist chooses price in market
two below the $\pi^2 = 0$ contour; no firm specializing
in product 2 can undercut him and earn nonnegative
profit. And regulatory policies will not be
useful to move the monopolist to bc, because we
assume the regulator can dictate prices for
product one only. If the regulator could do more
than this, then deregulation of market two is not
genuine. The upshot is that any prices in the
cross-hatched area are sustainable under partial
regulation. A formal definition of this concept
is given below.

To be more specific about the prices a two-
product monopolist will choose within the cross-
hatched area, assumptions about regulatory
policies are needed. For example, suppose
initially the monopolist is protected from
entrants in both markets by the regulator, and
prices are given by point r, the Ramsey prices.
Then suppose that only market two is totally

deregulated, that is, the regulator abandons both price and entry regulation in market two, while maintaining what was a Ramsey price in market one. The monopolist would move from r to point r' where profit is at a maximum subject to the market one price. At r' there is no cross subsidy and the monopolist is safe from entrant firms, although profit is positive.

Alternatively, suppose before deregulation the monopolist operates at point d where profit is zero and there is a cross subsidy from product one to product two. The cross subsidy is viable owing to regulatory entry barriers. Under the same form of deregulation, the monopolist would move to point d' where the cross subsidy persists but profit is now positive. The cross subsidy remains viable owing to entry regulation in market one.

On the other hand, a cross subsidy from product two to product one cannot persist after deregulation. If point a represents the initial before deregulation prices, then after deregulation if the monopolist moves along the vertical dashed line below point a, he cannot thwart entry into market two. In fact, without a change in regulatory policy allowing a higher price for product one, the two-product monopoly cannot survive.

Finally, Figure 4-1 suggests possibilities for monopoly expansion. If initially there are two independent firms, and the first is regulated and held to zero profit while the second is unregulated, the starting point lies at some point along segment fk where firm two's profit is at a maximum. If the first firm is now allowed to enter unregulated markets, it can operate just below point f and drive firm two out of business. This possibility of regulated firms entering unregulated markets is of great concern to regulators. Their fears are realized at point f. The irony is that a two-product monopolist operating at point f is superior to having two

independent monopolists. That is, point f is on a
higher welfare contour than any point within area
fghk where independent firms could survive. Thus
the regulator's fear that one firm might drive out
the other and lower overall welfare is unfounded.

More generally, we have just enumerated several
undesirable results of partial regulation
including positive profit, persistence of cross
subsidies, and lower welfare. But these results
stem from a policy (scenario 3) that is misguided
at the outset.[7] In our example, the two-product
firm is a natural monopoly and should be the only
firm in both markets based on efficiency
arguments. If the natural monopoly is sustainable
and both markets contestable, regulation can be
avoided. If there are entry barriers in both
markets, regulation is necessary to attain a
second-best outcome. However, if only one market
is contestable, partial regulation is not the
answer; it is strictly inferior to total
regulation.

Partial Regulation versus Total Regulation

There are caveats which must accompany the
conclusion that partial regulation is strictly
inferior to total regulation. First, the analysis
has assumed optimum regulatory policies. In
scenario one, the regulator maximized social
welfare subject to a break-even constraint on the
monopolist, and the result was second-best or
Ramsey prices. But would the regulator want to
pursue this policy, and, if so, could, the
regulator pursue this policy? Whether regulators
would want to, is related to the theme of this
book. Regulators may have their own agenda, one
that may not conform to the benign, welfare-
maximizing paradigm. Becker (Chapter 2), Yandle
(Chapter 3) and many other writers depict
regulators as being responsive to political
pressure groups. These groups will attempt to

influence regulatory decisions in their favor by
providing political support (e.g., campaign
contributions or votes) to the regulator.
Naturally the better organized, wealthier pressure
groups will be more influential (Stigler 1971),
and their agenda are not likely to be social
welfare maximization.

But suppose the regulator is intent on
maximizing social welfare. Can it be done?
Unfortunately, the answer is no in many instances
owing to incomplete information. To calculate
Ramsey prices, for example, the regulator requires
information on demand elasticities, cross
elasticities and marginal costs. Good estimates
of these measures often are unavailable, or
perhaps available only to the firms. But firms
have incentives to misrepresent the information,
given that they are among the pressure groups.
Thus regulators frequently are confronted with
making decisions under incomplete information, and
even the well-intentioned regulator may appear to
be responsive to pressure groups, if these groups
are the chief sources of information.

The second caveat for the conclusion that
partial regulation is strictly inferior to total
regulation concerns the cost of regulating. In
scenario one, regulation was implicitly assumed
costless. But there are two sources of cost that
cannot be ignored. First is the administrative
cost of running the regulatory agency. Depending
on the size of the state or the jurisdictions of
the state or federal agencies, these costs can be
substantial. Second is the distortions that
regulation may introduce. The classic example of
this is the Averch-Johnson overcapitalization bias
associated with rate-of-return regulation.

The third caveat concerns technology. In
Figure 4-1, the profit contours were stationary,
reflecting a world of unchanging costs. But costs
do change with changes in technology. A priori,
we cannot say how a technological change will

shift the profit contours of the single-product
firms relative to the contours of the two-product
firm. The cost advantages of having a single firm
may increase, decrease or completely vanish. The
important point, however, is whether having a two-
product, regulated natural monopoly or two,
single-product competitors is more conducive to
innovation. Theoretically, arguments could be
made to support either market structure as the
more innovative, which would prompt us to examine
the evidence. But the evidence is difficult to
interpret. For example, since the AT&T breakup,
innovation in telecommunications has been rapid.
Is this due to competition? Is this due to a
partially deregulated AT&T? Could this have come
about without the breakup, but with alternative
regulatory policies?
     The point is that partial regulation is
strictly inferior to total regulation, if we make
simplifying assumptions about perfect information,
costless regulation and constant technologies.
Relaxing one or more assumptions may alter the
inferiority of partial regulation, because total
regulation may appear less attractive. Of course,
total regulation's potentially unattractive
features with respect to imperfect information,
regulatory costs and lack of innovation also apply
to partial regulation in some degree. If these
features plague total regulation, we cannot rule
out that they also plague partial regulation. In
the remainder of the paper, these features will be
downplayed on the premise that they are equally
likely to effect partial and total regulation.
The efficacy of partial regulation will be
discussed as it was in the previous section; that
is, in terms of profit, welfare and cross
subsidies.

Sustainability Under Partial Regulation

     If a totally regulated, multiproduct firm is

partially deregulated, will it continue to produce
the same set of outputs? Will it abandon some of
the markets where there is new competition? Will
it divest into new markets? To shed light on
these issues, we appeal to the sustainability
concept. For instance, if sustainable prices
exist for a totally regulated firm, then we might
expect that they would also exist if the firm
became partially regulated. And, if so, the firm
probably would have an incentive to continue
producing all the same outputs, and possibly add
new ones. Alternatively, if sustainable prices do
not exist for a totally regulated firm, then we
might expect that they would not exist if the firm
became partially regulated. But this turns out to
be incorrect. A partially regulated firm is
protected from entry in one or more markets, and
it can take advantage of this by charging higher
prices in protected markets, while possibly cross
subsidizing the competitive markets.

Thus, whether or not a partially-regulated firm
is sustainable will depend on the regulatory
environment. To capture this, we introduce the
notion of sustainable under partial regulation
(SUPR). We will compare SUPR to sustainability,
and we will concentrate on necessary conditions
for a firm to be SUPR. For example, we know that
zero profit is a necessary condition for
sustainability, but we show that it is not
necessary for SUPR. This result and others that
are derived below mean that the market forces
keeping an unregulated firm in check, namely
contestability, will not keep a partially
regulated firm in check. Consequently, monitoring
partially regulated firms is becoming one of the
more important dilemmas confronting regulators.

Consider a multiproduct firm producing output
vector $q = (q_1, \ldots, q_n)$ at prices $p = (p_1, \ldots, p_n)$.
Demand for the ith good is written $q_i(p)$ and is
assumed to be continuously differentiable with
$\partial q_i / \partial p_i < 0$ and $\partial q_i / \partial p_j \geq 0$ for $i, j = 1, \ldots, n$,

$i \neq j$. Thus the n goods are weak gross
substitutes. The firm's total cost is given by
the continuously differentiable function $C(q)$
defined for $q \geq 0$, and marginal costs are denoted
$MC_i = \partial C(q)/\partial q_i$, $i = 1,...n$.
   Initially, the firm is assumed to have a
monopoly in all n markets. Profit is given by

$$\pi(p) \equiv pq(p) - C(q(p))$$

$$\equiv \sum_{i \in N} p_i q_i(p) - C(q_1(p),...,q_n(p)) \qquad (1)$$

where N is the set of all n goods. $\pi(p)$ is
continuous by continuity of the demand and cost
functions and is assumed to be strictly concave
with a unique maximum attained at p* such that
$\pi(p*) > 0$. The firm is regulated in all markets
by a single regulator. Regulation is effective by
constraining the firm to zero profit and by
preventing entry into all markets. Whether the
monopolist is sustainable is immaterial in this
initial setting. Regardless of how inefficient
the monopolist might be or the extent of cross
subsidization among products, new firms cannot
compete if the regulator is effective in
disallowing entry. However, if the no entry
policy is relaxed in a proper subset of the n
markets, sustainability becomes an issue for this
partially regulated monopolist.
   For convenience, order the goods so that the
set of markets $R = \{1,...,r\}$ continues to be
regulated while the set of markets $N-R =
\{r+1,...,n\}$ is unregulated. The price vector for
the monopolist is denoted by $p^m = (\bar{p}^m_1,
...,\bar{p}^m_r, p^m_{r+1},...,p^m_n)$, where the bar notation
indicates that prices in the first r markets are
set by the regulator, perhaps after some review
process. At this point we will not specify how
these prices are set, but sustainability of the
monopolist will certainly be dependent on the

method used.

A firm that attempts to enter one or more of the unregulated markets charges prices p^e and has the same production technology available to it as does the monopolist. If the monopoly is invulnerable to all potential entry, then it is said to be SUPR.

Definition. The monopoly price vector $p^m = (\overline{p}^m_1, \ldots, \overline{p}^m_r, p^m_{r+1}, \ldots, p^m_n)$ is sustainable under partial regulation (SUPR), if and only if, given the regulated prices $\overline{p}^m_i$, $i \in R$, $p^e_s y^e_s - C(y^e_s) < 0$, and $\pi(p^m) \geq 0$, $p^e_s < p^m_s$, and $y^e_s \leq q^s(p^e_s, p^m_{N-s})$ for all $S \subseteq N-R$.

This definition is based on the Panzar and Willig definition of sustainability, the distinction being that firms can only enter markets in N-R: they are barred by regulatory fiat from entry into markets in R. A successful entrant must undercut the monopolist's price in one or more of the markets open for entry and earn nonegative profit. Note too, that an entrant need only serve a portion of market demand; that is, there is no common carrier constraint in the unregulated markets.

Sustainability of a firm depends on the firm's costs, the potential rivals' costs, and the market demands: it is defined independent of any regulatory environment. SUPR on the other hand, is defined relative to a particular regulatory environment, and a firm that is SUPR in one environment may not be SUPR in another. Consequently, we must specify the environment in order to examine the properties of SUPR; the more pervasive the environment specified, the more useful the concept is for policy analysis.

Under total regulation, an often studied environment has the regulator maximizing welfare while holding the firm to zero profit. The equivalent action in a partially regulated setting

would seem to be that the firm can choose any
prices in the unregulated markets, but prices in
the regulated markets must yield zero profit
while satisfying some welfare measure. But
separating the regulated and unregulated markets
for the purpose of determining profits is
arbitrary if common costs are involved. Because
common costs are prevalent in partially regulated
firms, another assumption about regulatory
behavior is needed. The following assumption
would seem to provide a natural starting point for
the regulator, particularly since information
requirements are minimal.

Assumption 1. Initially, the firm is totally
regulated in all n markets, prices are
undominated, and profit is zero. Under partial
regulation, price and entry constraints are lifted
in markets $r+1,\ldots,n$; but in markets $1,\ldots,r$
prices are assumed to remain at their initial,
zero profit levels and regulatory entry barriers
continue in force.[8]

The monopolist, with new found latitude after
deregulation, attempts to maximize profit subject
to the set prices in the regulated markets.
However, the monopolist is assumed to be aware of
potential entrants, and he attempts to choose
prices that will deter entry. The monopolist's
problem can be written

$$\text{maximize} \atop p_{r+1},\ldots,p_n \qquad \pi^m \;=\; \sum_{i=1}^{r} \overline{p}^m_i q^m_i(\overline{p}^m_R, p^m_{N-R})$$

$$+ \sum_{i=r+1}^{n} p^m_i q^m_i(\overline{p}^m_R, p^m_{N-R})$$

$$- C(q^m_R(\cdot), q^m_{N-R}(\cdot)) \tag{2}$$

subject to $p^e_s y^e_s < C(y^e_s)$, for all $S \subseteq N-R$, (3)

$p^e_s < p^m_s$ and $y^e_s \leq q^S$ $(\overline{p}^m_R, p^m_{N-R-S}, p^e_s)$ (4)

If a solution to this problem exists with $\pi^m \geq 0$, then the monopolist is SUPR. Constraints given by (3) and (4) ensure that the monopolist will not choose prices that can be successfully undercut by entrants.

We can now introduce several properties of SUPR.

Property 1. If the firm's totally regulated prices are sustainable (implying that the firm is a natural monopoly), then its partially regulated prices will be SUPR and profit will be positive.[9]

Any sustainable price vector is SUPR, this is obvious from the definitions. However, a monopolist charging sustainable prices under total regulation can raise price in at least one market after deregulation, earn positive profit, and be SUPR. This can be seen by referring to Figure 4-1. Prior to partial deregulation the firm is using a sustainable price vector, implying that it is operating somewhere along arc bc. If market 2 is deregulated, the firm can always raise price in market 2, holding the price in market 1 constant, without moving above the zero profit contour of a potential entrant into market 2. How far the firm can raise price and still be SUPR depends on the starting point along arc bc.

Property 2. If the totally regulated firm is a nonsustainable natural monopoly, then whether or not the firm is SUPR depends on which markets are deregulated. Also, cross subsidization may or may not persist after deregulation.

Figure 4-1 illustrates that a sustainable natural monopoly, starting with sustainable

prices, will always be SUPR. Figure 4-2
illustrates a nonsustainable natural monopoly that
charges prices given by point r prior to
deregulation. If market 2 only is entry
deregulated, the firm will not be SUPR because
another firm can successfully enter market two by
charging any price between p_2' and p_2''. However,
if only market 1 is totally deregulated, the
nonsustainable natural monopoly is SUPR because it
is not vulnerable in market 1. A cross subsidy
from market 2 to market 1 is also possible in this
case.

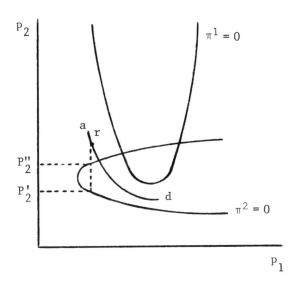

Figure 4-2

Property 3.   A natural monopoly is not
necessary for SUPR.

This can be easily demonstrated with a
numerical example.   In a two-product case, let
demands be independent and given by $q_1(p) = -.5p_1$
$+ 10$, $q_2(p) = -1.4p_2 + 20$, and cost be given by
$C(q_1(p),q_2(p)) = 5q_1 + 4q_2 + .44q_1q_2 - 24$.   These
functions give rise to Figure 4-3 where the
undominated portion of the zero profit contour for
the two-product monopolist is labelled $\pi^{12} = 0$,
and single-product firm 1 (2) earns nonnegative
profit in the interval $p_1' \le p_1 \le p_1''$ ($p_2' \le p_2 \le$
p_2'').   At (p_1',p_2') we have $C(q_1(p_1),q_2(p_2)) >$
$C(q_1(p_1),0) + C(0,q_2(p_2))$, implying there are
diseconomies of scope.   Therefore, the cost
function is not subadditive and the firm is not a
natural monopoly.   If market two is deregulated

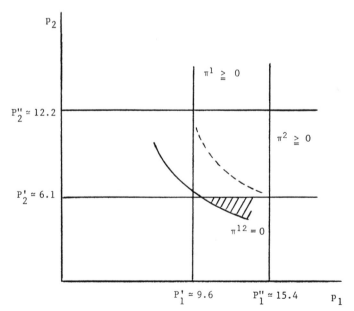

Figure 4-3

and market one is not, the two-product monopolist
is SUPR at any price vector in the hatched area.
This non natural monopolist can earn positive
profit and be SUPR while cross subsidizing the
unregulated market. Partial regulation is
protecting a production technology with
diseconomies.

There is a limit, however, to the extent that
diseconomies can persist under partial regulation
before entry occurs. To illustrate this, we
derive a sufficient condition for a firm not be be
SUPR which is instructive in showing the market
and production forces at work. In Figure 4-3, if
the undominated zero-profit contour for the two-
product firm is the dashed curve, the firm cannot
be SUPR.[10] Continuing with market one as the
regulated market, the dashed curve must not cut
below the lower segment of the $\pi_2 = 0$ contour.
This follows if

$$p^m_2 q_2(p^m) > C(0, q_2(p^m))$$ (5)

for all undominated p such that

$$p^m_1 q_1(p^m) + p^m_2 q_2(p^m) = C(q_1(p^m), q_2(p^m)).$$ (6)

Together, (5) and (6) imply

$$p^m_1 q_1(p^m) < C(q_1(p^m), q_2(p^m)) - C(0, q_2(p^m)),$$

or product one covers less than its marginal cost.
Rewriting this last inequality as

$$p^m_1 < \frac{C(q_1(p^m), q_2(p^m)) - C(0, q_2(p^m))}{q_1(p^m)}$$ (7)

we can view both sides of (7) as functions of p^m_1.
If (7) holds for all undominated p^m_1, then the
firm cannot be SUPR. A sufficient condition for
this is that (7) holds for all p_1 such that $0 \le p_1$

$\leq p^{m*}_1$, where p^{m*}_1 is the largest undominated value of p^m_1. But at $p_1 = 0$, inequality (7) holds because the right side is clearly positive provided that $q_1(0,p_2)$ is finite. As p_1 increases from zero to p^{m*}_1, if the partial derivative of the right side is no less than one (which is the slope of the left side function), the inequality holds throughout. The condition on this partial is

$$q_1 < [MC_2 - MC^0_2] \frac{\partial q_2}{\partial p_1}$$

$$+ [MC_1 - \frac{C(q_1(p), q_2(p)) - C(0, q_2(p))}{q_1}] \frac{\partial q_1}{\partial p_1} \qquad (8)$$

where $MC^0_2 = \partial C(0, q_2(p))/\partial q_2$.

Expression (8) reveals the properties guaranteeing that a firm is not SUPR. In the first term on the right side, $\partial q_2/\partial p_1$ is nonnegative by the weak gross substitute assumption. Therefore, a positive bracketed term contributes to the desired result. This follows if there are negative cost complimentarities in production, or marginal cost rises as new products are added. Similarly, since $\partial q_1/\partial p_1 < 0$, a negative second bracketed term contributes to the desired result. This bracketed term is the rate of change of average incremental cost (See Panzar and Willig 1977); therefore, declining average incremental cost favors the firm not being SUPR. The combination of negative cost complimentarities and declining average incremental cost, when multiplied by the appropriate partial, must exceed some threshold level of q_1 on the left side of (8).

The intuition goes as follows. Suppose the firm is charging a relatively low price in the regulated market and finds itself vulnerable to entrants in the unregulated market. If the firm is permitted to raise the regulated price, it will do so in order to increase regulated revenues which will then permit a lower price in the competitive market. However, this strategy may fail if the greater output sold in the unregulated market can only be produced at ever increasing costs (the negative cost complimentarities), and the advantages of large scale production are eroded in the regulated market as output in that market decreases with the higher price (the declining average incremental cost).

The point of this exercise is to illustrate that a firm may need to exhibit rather strong non natural monopoly properties before we can be certain that it is not SUPR. In turn, this implies that partial regulation may be a means of protecting very inefficient production. But even if the partially regulated firm is a natural monopoly, we are likely to observe positive profit and possibly cross subsidies. The fundamental problem is in the partial regulation approach. If a firm is a natural monopoly and only some of its markets are contestable, opening those markets to competition may only mean higher profit for the monopoly with little, if any, entry. Alternatively, if a firm is not a natural monopoly, or if it once was but no longer is owing to new technologies, then partial regulation may be less desirable than either total deregulation or breaking the firm up. This latter option is sometimes attempted in a nominal fashion through separation procedures.

Separation Procedures

A common attempt to solve the problems presented by partially regulated firms is to simply separate the firm's markets. This is accomplished using accounting techniques that allocate the firm's total revenue and cost between the regulated and unregulated products. But where common costs are involved, allocation or separations procedures are a hopelessly arbitrary approach that can lead to undesirable prices and cross subsidies.[11] In addition, there is the danger that among some regulators, separations procedures may foster an unwarranted feeling of accomplishment.

Sweeney (1982) explores the problems with separation procedures for a partially regulated firm. The regulator requires each product in the regulated set to cover no more than its allocated cost. As in the previous section, we assume that products in the set $R = (1,...,r)$ are regulated while those in the set $N-R = (r+1,...,n)$ are not. To account for the common costs that are to be allocated, we write the cost function as

$$\sum_{i=1}^{r} C_i(q_i) + \sum_{i=r+1}^{n} C_i(q_i) + F \qquad (9)$$

where $C_i(q_i)$ is the direct cost for product i and F is the common cost.[12] Each product must cover no more than its direct cost plus its share of common cost, or

$$p_i q_i(p) \leq C_i(q_i(p)) + \alpha_i F, \qquad i \in R \qquad (10)$$

where α_i is the common cost allocator for product i. We assume $0 < \alpha_i < 1$ meaning that each regulated product must cover some part of

common cost, and $\sum_{i=1}^{r} \alpha_i < 1$ because some common

cost gets allocated to the unregulated products.

A number of different allocations are considered by Sweeney, but we will confine ourselves to just one which will be sufficient to illustrate the important results. We will assume that α_i is a differentiable function of the outputs in R,

$$\alpha_i = \alpha_i(q_1, \ldots, q_r) \tag{11}$$

with partials

$$\frac{\partial \alpha_i}{\partial q_i} > 0, \quad i=1,\ldots,r \tag{12}$$

$$\frac{\partial \alpha_i}{\partial q_j} < 0, \quad i,j=1,\ldots r, i \neq j. \tag{13}$$

Thus, as the ith output increases, more of the common cost is allocated to it and less is allocated to all other outputs in R. The monopolist's problem can be written as

$$\max_{p_i, \ldots, p_n} \pi = \sum_{i=1}^{r} [p_i q_i(p) - C(q_i)]$$

$$+ \sum_{i=r+1}^{n} [p_i q_i(p) - C_i(q_i)] - F \tag{14}$$

subject to $p_i q_i(p) - C_i(q_i(p))$

$$- \alpha_i(q(p))F \leq 0, \quad i \epsilon R \tag{15}$$

$$0 \leq p_i \leq \hat{p}_i, \quad i \epsilon N \tag{16}$$

where $\hat{p}_i$ is an upper bound on price, or the price that would drive demand to zero.

The difference between this problem and the problem presented in the previous section is noteworthy. In the latter, the prices in markets $1,\ldots,r$ were set by the regulator, and the monopolist could only choose the prices in markets $r+1,\ldots,n$. In effect, the regulator adopted a separations procedure, which was left unspecified, and using that procedure she set prices which

ostensibly satisfied some regulatory goal.
However, in the above problem, a separations
procedure is specified, and then the monopolist is
free to set all n prices within the confines of
the procedure. A priori, we cannot say which
approach is preferable without further specifying
the information available to both the monopolist
and the regulator.
    Returning to the problem given by (14) - (16),
Sweeney derives two important results shown
graphically in Figure 4-4. Assuming that market
one is again the regulated market, the solution to
problem (14) - (16) can be represented by point a.
Curve aa' represents constraint (15) which Sweeney
shows to have the general shape as illustrated.
The monopolist maximizes profit along this
constraint by locating at the highest isoprofit
contour which has at least one point in common
with aa'. Sweeney's two results are that prices
at point a are dominated, and that price in the
unregulated market exceeds the unconstrained

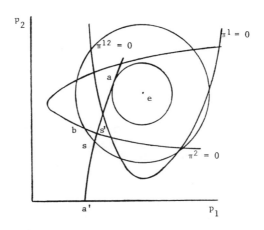

Figure 4-4

profit maximizing price corresponding to point e.
These results obviously do not bode well for this
separations approach: it yields prices such that
one or more of them can be lowered to improve
welfare without decreasing the monopolist's
profit, and prices in unregulated markets are
high.

In one sense, these results may appeal to
regulators, because the prices are high in the
unregulated markets, thereby quelling fears of
cross subsidies from the regulated markets.
Moreover, competitors in unregulated markets
should be pleased that the monopolist is
apparently not relying on profits in the regulated
markets to predatory price in their markets. In
fact, referring again to Figure 4-4, a single-
output firm can successfully enter market two
given the monopolist's choice of point a. In
other words, point a is not SUPR.

The firm has chosen a high price and low output
in the unregulated market so that more of the
common cost can be shifted to the regulated
market. However, in doing this, the unregulated
market has been left vulnerable to entrants. The
advantages of natural monopoly production are then
lost.

The monopolist may not behave passively towards
potential entrants, however. If he is aware of
the potential and of his competitors technologies,
then he can append constraints given by (3) to the
problem in (14) - (16). Now he prices according
to the separations procedures, while at the same
time preventing entry by ensuring that the
unregulated prices are not too high. In Figure 4-
4, the monopolist constrained to operate along aa'
by the separations procedure is SUPR along ss'.
To maximize profit he would choose point s', the
solution to problem (14) - (16) after (3) is
appended.

Conclusion

Deregulation has moved swiftly but not completely into regulated industries in the U.S. The result is partial regulation: a system that has firms operating in both regulated and competitive markets. All this has occurred before any set of coherent policies toward these newly structured firms was developed. The result is that regulators and firms are groping for ways to address issues that they never before confronted. Issues including how to price products where there is some competition, when should entry into markets be encouraged or discouraged, how can cross subsidies from regulated to unregulated markets be avoided, and simply how to revamp an obsolete regulatory structure.

In this chapter a framework for addressing some of these problems has been introduced. Two major determinants for setting regulatory policies are whether or not a firm is a natural monopoly and whether or not there are barriers to entry into the firm's markets. With these in mind the SUPR concept was used to illustrate the undesirable consequences of partial regulation. For examples, a partially regulated natural monopoly earns positive profit, or a partially regulated non natural monopoly is sustainable. Neither result would be anticipated under total regulation or total deregulation. One reason for the undesirable results of partial regulation is the impossibility of allocating common costs across multiple products.

Will partial regulation give way to total deregulation, reregulation, or will it continue more or less as is? Most economists would argue that the answer should be grounded in economic efficiency; that is, which tack yields the greatest improvement in efficiency. But the answer will also depend on pressure group activities and the political philosophies of all

three branches of government. Thus economic
efficiency may occupy a secondary role.[13]
Considerably more research will be required if
economists are to have an influence on policies
involving important and rapidly changing
industries.

Notes

1. I am indebted to Gary Becker, Robert Hahn, Charles Mason, and Jason Shogren
for helpful comments. Responsibility for errors is mine alone.
2. See Berg and Tschirhart (1988, Chapters 2 and 7) for a summary of these
conditions.
3. Figure 1 can be generated by demand curves

$$q_1 = -0.2p_1 + 0.1p_2 + 10$$

$$q_2 = -0.3p_2 + 0.1p_1 + 12$$

where q_i and p_i, i=1,2, are quantities and prices, and by cost functions

$$C(q_1,q_2) = 0.8q_1 + q_2 + 270$$

for positive q_1 and q_2, and

$$C(0,q_2) = 1.2q_2 + 140$$

$$C(q_1,0) = q_1 + 150.$$

4. A natural monopoly results when one firm can produce the desired outputs
less expensively than multiple firms. A necessary and sufficient condition for
natural monopoly is that the firm's cost function exhibit subadditivity of costs
over the relevant region of outputs. Thus,

$$C(q^1 +...+ q^m) < C(q^1)+...+C(q^m)$$

for any m output vectors, where $q^i = (q^i_1,...,q^i_n)$ is the ith output vector and
there are n outputs.
5. Undominated prices are those such that no price can be lowered, ceteris
paribus, without decreasing profit. Panzar and Willig (1977) provide a set of
necessary conditions for sustainability.
6. If the monopolist charged prices given by point a, for example, an entrant
in market two could undercut the monopolist by charging a price along the dotted
line. The entrant would earn positive profit. Prices at point a exhibit cross
subsidization from market two to market one, because consumers in market two are
paying more than the stand-alone cost of serving them.
7. Baumol (1981) makes this point about a similar environment.
8. For example, the initial prices could be Ramsey prices.
9. This follows by continuity of the demand and cost function. Let $\bar{p}^m_N$ =
$(\bar{p}^m_1,...,\bar{p}^m_n)$ be the totally regulated prices which are sustainable. After
deregulation, the monopolist can charge $(\bar{p}^m_R, \bar{p}^m_{N-R}) = (\bar{p}^m_1,...,$

$\bar{p}^m{}_r, \bar{p}^m{}_{r+1}, \ldots, \bar{p}^m{}_{r+i} + \delta, \ldots, \bar{p}^m{}_n)$ for $i = 1, \ldots, n-r$, and for $\delta > 0$. Because the totally regulated prices earned zero profit and were undominated, it must be that $\pi(\bar{p}^m{}_R, \bar{p}^m{}_{N-R}) > 0$. Moreover, by continuity, δ can be chosen sufficiently small so that potential entrants still earn negative profit;

$$p^e{}_S \, y^e{}_S < C(y^e{}_S(\cdot))$$

for all $S \subseteq N-R$, $p^e{}_S < p^m{}_S$ and $y^e{}_S \leq q^S \, (\bar{p}^m{}_R, p^m{}_{N-R-S}, p^e{}_S)$.

10. Baseman (1981) makes use of this same diagram to illustrate a similar point.

11. See Braeutigam (1980) for an analysis of fully-distributed-cost pricing.

12. Cabe (1988) uses a more general cost function where the variable costs depend on the level of fixed costs. This alters a number of Sweeney's results.

13. In Becker's (1983) theory of interest group pressure for political influence, economic efficiency can be enhanced through interest group pressure, because policies promoting efficiency are more likely to be adopted.

References

Baseman, Kenneth C., "Open Entry and Cross-Subsidization in Regulated Markets," in Studies in Public Regulation, ed. Gary Fromm, Cambridge, Mass: MIT Press, 1981, 329-360.

Baumol, William J., "Comment on Open Entry and Cross-Subsidization in Regulated Markets," in Studies in Public Regulation, ed. Gary Fromm, Cambridge, Mass: MIT Press, 1981, 361-364.

_____, "On the Proper Cost Tests for Natural Monopoly in a Multiproduct Industry," American Economic Review 67 (December 1977): 809-22.

_____, Elizabeth E. Bailey and Robert D. Willig, "Weak Invisible Hand Theorems on the Sustainability of Prices in Multiproduct Monopoly," American Economic Review 67 (1977): 350-65.

_____, John C. Panzar and Robert D. Willig, Contestable Markets: and the Theory of Industry Structure, New York: Harcourt Brace Jovanovich, Inc., 1982.

Becker, Gary S., "A Theory of Competition Among Pressure Groups for Political Influence," Quarterly Journal of Economics 98 (1983): 371-400.

_____, "Political Competition among Interest Groups," in The Political Economy of Government

  Regulation, ed. Jason F. Shogren, Norwell, Mass:
  Kluwer Academic Publishers, 1989.
Berg, Sanford V. and John Tschirhart, Natural
  Monopoly Regulation: Principles and Practice,
  New York: Cambridge University Press, 1988.
Braeutigam, Ronald R. "An Analysis of Fully
  Distributed Cost Pricing in Regulated
  Industries," Bell Journal of Economics 11 (1980):
  1982-96.
Cabe, Richard A. "Rate of Return Regulation of
  Multiproduct Firms," Ph.D. dissertation,
  University of Wyoming, 1988.
Panzar, John C. and Robert D. Willig, "Free Entry
  and the Sustainability of Natural Monopoly," Bell
  Journal of Economics 8 (Spring 1977): 1-22.
Stigler, George J. "The Theory of Economic
  Regulation," Bell Journal of Economics 2 (1971):
  3-21.
Sweeney, G. "Welfare Implications of Fully
  Distributed Cost Pricing Applied to Partially
  Regulated Firms," Bell Journal of Economics 13
  (1982): 525-33.
Yandle, Bruce, "Bootleggers and Baptists in the
  Market for Regulation," in The Political Economy
  of Government Regulation, ed. Jason F. Shogren,
  Norwell, Mass: Kluwer Academic Publishers, 1989.

5

THE POLITICAL ECONOMY OF RISK COMMUNICATION POLICIES FOR FOOD AND ALCOHOLIC BEVERAGES

W. Kip Viscusi

Introduction

The 1980s have witnessed the emergence of hazard warning policies as a major component in efforts to promote product safety and job safety. Government agencies have launched sweeping efforts to label all carcinogenic risks in the workplace as well as to promote labeling for a wide variety of consumer products. In an extreme case, the state of California has promulgated regulations that hazard warnings be given for all significant exposures to carcinogens and reproductive toxicants generated by exposures to food, environmental conditions, and conditions at the workplace. Whereas the regulatory efforts of the 1970s focused primarily on technological solutions and engineering controls to safety problems, in the 1980s there has been a dramatic shift toward the increased use of warnings. The objective has been to augment technological controls with precautionary behavior on the part of the individuals exposed to the risks.

From a theoretical standpoint, hazard warning programs have much to recommend them. One of the major sources of market failure that has long been cited by economists has been a lack of information in situations in which individuals are making decisions under uncertainty. Because of this lack of information, individuals may buy goods for which they are not fully cognizant of the risks, or they may accept jobs whose implications are not well understood before beginning work on it. Hazard warning efforts can eliminate this source of market failure directly by eliminating the information gap that exists.

In general, if one excludes the role of anxiety, this information will only be useful from an economic standpoint to the extent that it will potentially alter an individual's decisions. Two classes of decisions can be distinguished. The first consists of threshold choices in which an individual chooses whether or not to participate in an activity or purchase a particular good. The second type of behavioral choice pertains to precautionary behavior given that an individual has chosen to engage in a risky activity. Thus, warnings for a consumer product can have a twofold purpose in that they can alert the individual as to whether or not he or she should purchase the product and, if the individual does choose to purchase the good, the hazard warning can provide information regarding its proper use.

In addition to being a policy tool that can potentially remedy some of the market failures that have been noted by economists, hazard warnings raise other economic issues as well. In particular, society's objective with hazard warnings should not be to promote risk reduction at any cost or to interfere with informed decisions. Rather, it should be to provide individuals with information that will enable them to make sound economic decisions that enhance economic efficiency. Many warnings, for example, are not directed at providing risk information but instead are intended to provide

guidance with respect to proper use, such as
whether or not one should wear rubber gloves when
using drain opener. To the extent that one is
advising individuals of appropriate courses of
precautionary action, it is important to assess
whether the expected benefits associated with
these precautions are in excess of the expected
costs that are imposed on the individuals taking
the precautions. Thus, to the extent that we are
providing guidance rather than information,
one must ascertain whether this guidance is
appropriate from an efficiency standpoint.
  Hazard warning programs also raise another
class of economic issues pertaining to the
appropriate role of informational forms of
regulations. The first of these regulatory issues
pertains to the circumstances under which it is
appropriate to substitute a hazard warnings
program for direct forms of government regulation.
Any judgment along these lines depends in large
part upon the efficacy of hazard warnings in
providing information that is needed, and at
present our research regarding this efficacy is
still in its infancy. Thus, we have
selective research results pertaining to
particular case studies where warnings have had
well identified effects, and we have
developed guidelines for the design of hazard
warning efforts, but these results are not so
specific as to enable us to obtain
generalized predictions as to the circumstances in
which we can be confident that hazard warnings
programs will necessarily be superior to more
direct forms of intervention.[1] Any such
judgments must still be prepared on an individual
basis taking into account the specific factors of
the contexts being considered.
  The second class of regulatory issues, which
will be one of the major concerns for this
chapter, is the degree to which the political
context influences the structure of regulation. A

considerable literature in regulatory economics
has documented the role of various forms of
capture theories, as the parties being regulated
often influence the structure of regulation to
advance their own interests.[2] Similar influences
enter in some informational contexts as well. For
example, leading chemical and petroleum firms had
hazard warnings in place before the advent of the
OSHA hazard communication system so that it was in
their interest to support national hazard warnings
regulations, particularly since the regulations
that were promulgated did not require that they
alter their existing hazard warning programs.

The more common political context of
informational policies is that consumer and public
interest influences are at work as well. These
political factors affect not only the adoption of
hazard warnings programs, but also their content.
Thus, the hazard warning language may not be the
result of a detailed study to select the most
effective risk communication mode but instead may
be the result of an effort to satisfy these
special interest groups that supported the hazard
warning effort. This contamination of
informational policies with political overtones
has led to serious distortions in the warnings
message, as I will document with two of the case
studies presented in this chapter: Federally-
proposed alcohol beverage warning legislation and
food cancer warning efforts in California.

Principles for the Design of Hazard Warning Programs

Ideally, one might wish to embark on a hazard
warning effort in which one simply provided the
individuals exposed to the risk with complete
information pertaining to the hazard as
well as appropriate precautions to reduce the
risk. In the case of chemical risks in
particular, this would be a quite daunting

task. Supporting scientific evidence regarding
these hazards is often quite extensive and cannot
be easily distilled into a single summary
statistic. Even if it could, the recipients of
the warnings would lack the scientific expertise
to process the information reliably. Thus, the
task of the hazard warning program is quite
different than simply providing information.
Rather, the task is to communicate knowledge in a
meaningful manner, and this is quite a different
undertaking.

In addition to the lack of scientific expertise
in the general population, there are also
important cognitive limitations. Two such
limitations are most noteworthy. First,
individuals have limited information processing
capabilities. The amount of information that
people can process reliably from a hazard warning
message is bounded by the cognitive capabilities
that individuals bring to bear to such tasks.
Second, there are also a number of inadequacies in
the manner in which individuals respond to the
risk and more generally to choices under
uncertainty. These inadequacies, which have often
been designated as forms of "irrationality" in
individual choice, govern the context in which
hazard warning programs will necessarily operate.
As a result, we want to design hazard warning
programs that will be effective given the
environment in which they will work so that the
hazard warning efforts should take such influences
into account.

Here I will outline six principles for the
establishment of a sound hazard communications
system. These principles are by no means
exhaustive, but they do highlight many of the most
pertinent concerns that should be reflected in the
design of a hazard warning effort. In subsequent
sections we will assess how particular warnings
efforts have failed, in large part because of
their violation of these guidelines.

1.   To be effective, warnings must convey new
      information either about risks or
      precautions.

The first principle for hazard warnings is that
to be successful a warning effort must provide new
knowledge, not simply reiterate existing
knowledge. Until recently, the general
view in the literature was that hazard warnings
programs were a failure.[3] The early hazard
warning efforts were not truly informational in
nature, but instead were more forms of persuasion.
Policies that simply serve to remind individuals
about a risk are reiterating information about the
risks apparently in the hope that they will
browbeat individuals into changing their behavior.
Such efforts have not proven to be successful.
    In particular, risk communication efforts that
come under the heading of "education campaigns"
generally is viewed as having little or no effect,
as Adler and Pittle (1984) have demonstrated.
The "buckle up for safety, buckle up" seatbelt
campaign, for example, is generally viewed as a
failure. In addition, even the highly touted
cigarette warnings effort has had no statistically
identifiable effect on smoking behavior above that
which can be associated with other public
information activities by the Surgeon General and
by the media. Similarly, efforts by the Consumer
Product Safety Commission to reduce fire-related
death rates through consumer education programs
"had no measurable effect on adults' knowledge of
burn hazards."[4] Moreover, the burn injury rate
among the participants in the policy "did not show
significant decreases in frequency and severity."[6]
    These disappointing results do not imply that
all informational efforts are doomed to failure.
Hazard warning programs for job risks do have the
desired effects when these efforts provide new
knowledge about the risks. The major forces
that determine the differing efficacy of warning

labels in the job context is the weight that
individuals placed on the new information they
receive, as compared with their prior
information. Thus, individuals act in a Bayesian
fashion in that they used their prior information
and the new information provided through the
hazard warning, and to the extent that the
warning gives new information it will have the
desired effect. One way to increase this
informational weight is to expand the content of
the warning message. A study of consumer
responses to risk information on household
chemical products and pesticide products indicated
that precautionary behavior is strongly related to
the amount of new risk information provided by the
hazard warning.[6] Hazard warning efforts are not
doomed to failure, as some of the more pessimistic
observers have claimed, but instead can be
successful by providing new knowledge in a
convincing manner.

2.   The most effective warnings indicate to
      consumers the risks that they face as well
      as the precautions they must take to alter
      the risk.

The purpose of hazard warnings is not to
dictate behavior but to provide guidance for
individuals to make informed decisions. If our
objective were to deprive individuals of their
choices, then we should be banning products or
limiting their use rather than providing risk
information. Thus, an element of choice is
necessarily involved before warnings can be
effective.

The informational requirements are consequently
twofold. First, we want to provide information
about the risk so that individuals will know the
payoff to them of their precautionary actions. In
particular, what adverse health outcomes or
adverse physical effects will be influenced by the

hazard warning effort?   Ideally, we would also
like to communicate information regarding
the probability that these effects could occur.
With the present stage of development of most
hazard warning systems, such probability
information is at best rudimentary. We often
attempt to indicate in a qualitative manner the
extent of the risk by, for example, noting that
this product "may cause" injury or illness. By
changing the wording, we can indicate different
degrees of riskiness. With the exception of some
warnings provided in pharmaceutical contexts,
where the recipient of the warning is a learned
intermediary (i.e., the physician), specific
quantitative information is generally not provided
about risks because it is not believed that
individuals have the capability to process the
information reliably.
   The second component of the hazard warning is
to indicate the precautions individuals should
take. Informing people of the risks can be
helpful in encouraging informed choice with
respect to a particular risk. In the more usual
circumstance, our objective is not to discourage
purchase but rather to either influence the amount
of consumption, as would be the case with
dosage information for pharmaceutical products, or
to affect precautions regarding the use of the
product once it is purchased. By providing
information with respect to precautions
and risks, individuals can link their behavior
with the risk reductions that will result from
this behavior, thus establishing an economic
incentive for them to take the desired course of
action. This approach is not only attractive from
an economic standpoint, but it also has desirable
properties from the standpoint of the psychology
of decision making under uncertainty.

   3.   On-product labels are most effective
         for limited information transfer.

The major aspect governing the nature of the label is the limitation on the amount of information that individuals can process. A considerable literature in economics is focused on "bounded rationality" in economic decisions, and the psychology and marketing literature has generated similar results as well.[7]

An analogous phenomenon in the warning context is that of "label clutter" and "information overload."[8] From the bounded rationality literature, it would appear likely that labels that with overly extensive risk information would not be effective in communicating an understandable risk message. The importance of this phenomenon remained in question until recently, in large part because the studies examining the role of information overload did not consider a wide range of labeling alternatives and did not utilize representative consumer groups.

A field study that we undertook for EPA (see Magat, Viscusi, and Huber 1988) in which the cluttered label was a pesticides label now in use generated quite striking results. It is an oversimplification to simply conclude that cluttered labels do not work. When we inundate individuals with risk information on a hazard warning label, they do get the message that the product is risky, perhaps in large part because they have adapted to the labeling vocabulary now in place, which often includes extensive and cluttered labels for risky products. The main difficulty from the standpoint of individual decisions is not that they do not regard the product as risky; rather, they do not know which particular precautions to take in response to the risk. The warning message consequently gets garbled as individuals are aware of the general character of the risks but not of the specific precautions that are needed to reduce the hazards.

There is a second inadequacy as well. As we increase the amount of risk information, there is a tradeoff in terms of the amount of other information that is retained. In our study, what we found is that once risk information was increased, there was less recall of the information regarding proper use of the product.[9] These shortcomings were of particular concern since it is generally believed by EPA officials that the main product risk has to do with inappropriate use rather than a failure to take precautions. Household pesticide products have been sufficiently diluted so that if they are used according to the directions they pose very little individual risk. However, if individuals use these pesticide products in the wrong concentration by, for example, not observing the appropriate mixture between the pesticide and water, then the concentrated form of the pesticide will pose potentially substantial risks. Our objective then should be to provide concise and clear risk information, recognizing that some redundancy may be an attractive feature, but that in general we should avoid the tendency to have a label that is so cluttered with risk information that individuals cannot make effective use of the information.

4.   Hazard warning programs should take into account individuals' cognitive limitations.

Another form of cognitive limitation that has been identified in a variety of studies both in the psychology literature and economics literature is that individual risk perceptions tend to be biased in a systematic fashion. In particular, individuals show a tendency to overestimate low probability events and underestimate high probability events.[10] For the typical hazard warning that deals with a low probability

event, what this behavioral pattern implies is
that individuals will tend to over-react to the
risk information by acting as if the true
probability associated with some risks is greater
than it actually is.

   This behavior is not a mysterious form of
irrationality, but is exactly what we would
predict from a Bayesian perspective. Figure 5-1
illustrates the nature of this updating process.
The situation in which individuals assess all
risks as being identical is given by the
horizontal prior assessment line. If risk
perceptions for the various risks coincided with
the actual risks of the product, then the risk
perceptions would fall on the 45 degree line as
indicated. In practice, what we observe is
that individual risk perceptions tend to be along

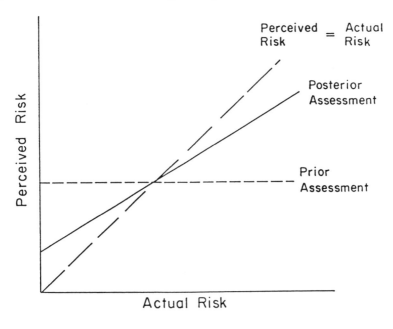

Figure 5-1

the intermediate posterior assessment line
indicated on the figure. Thus, individuals over-
assess the low probability events and
under-assess the higher probability events. From
a Bayesian perspective, the interpretation of this
phenomenon is that individuals learn from their
initial prior assessments, but this learning is
incomplete. In particular, whereas individuals
move toward the truth, their posterior assessment
line does not coincide with the 45 degree line
except in situations when full information
regarding the risks has been given and processed
by the individuals. If the risk information is
convincing, the posterior risk assessment line
will lie closer to the 45 degree line associated
with perfect risk information. Only when
individuals completely dismiss inaccurate prior
beliefs will risk perceptions lie on the 45 degree
line. This failure to learn is not necessarily an
inadequacy, but it does indicate that people
bring to bear previous knowledge when forming
their probabilistic beliefs. Moreover, a hazard
warning effort must be very persuasive to lead
individuals to alter their risk perceptions
since individuals may understandably place
substantial weight on their previous experiences
and past knowledge regarding a product.
     One implication of this phenomenon is that when
we provide people with risk information they will
tend to exaggerate the risk associated with it.
Thus, if we tell individuals that a product poses
a risk of one chance in two million, when they
process this information it will have a greater
effect on their risk perceptions than it should.
This phenomenon is illustrated by the data in
Table 5-1. This table reports on two different
studies of the price increases that individuals
would be willing to pay for products that involved
a reduced risk of injury. In situations in which
the risk reduction was quite modest (equal to
1/2,000,000 per year) the implicit values of the

Table 5-1

Injury Valuations at Different Risk Levels

Implicit Values for 1/2,000,000 Risk Change

Bleach:	$ Value/Injury
Chloramine gassing	300,000
Child poisoning	420,000
Drain opener:	
Hand burn	120,000
Child poisoning	360,000

Implicit Values for 5/10,000 Risk Change

Toilet Bowl Cleaner:	
Chloramine Gassing	912
Child Poisoning	1,010
Eyeburn	610
Insecticide:	
Skin Poisoning	1,233
Inhalation	1,428
Child Poisoning	2,860

health outcomes were quite substantial--in the hundreds of thousands of dollars. In contrast, for a different and more severe group of risks for which the risk changes were 5/10,000, the implicit valuations per unit risk reduction were several orders of magnitude smaller. In addition, there is one health outcome in common in both sets of experiments--chloramine gassing--and in the case where the risk change was 1/2,000,000 this outcome had an implicit value of $300,000, whereas with the risk change of 5/10,000 the valuation was only $912. Thus, the tendency to respond in an exaggerated economic manner to low probability events was borne out.

A similar phenomenon capturing related aspects of risk perceptions is presented in Table 5-2.

That table gives the willingness to pay for
successive risk reductions of 5/10,000 for
different pairs of injury. What is noteworthy is
that individual willingness to pay for the risk
reductions initially diminishes. The first risk
reduction at a base level of risk of 15/10,000 is
valued much more greatly than the risk reduction
when the starting risk level was 10/10,000, but
what is particularly striking is that the last
risk reduction that begins at 5/10,000 and which
takes the risk to zero is valued at an increasing
amount. Rather than having a diminishing risk
valuation as the extent of the risk reduction is
increased, for the final risk reduction that leads
to complete certainty there is a dramatic jump in
the valuation. This phenomenon is to be expected
since as we see from Table 5-1 the chance of very
low probability events will be greatly
exaggerated. Once we take the risk to zero there
will be an incremental drop in the probability
that reflects the character of risk perceptions.
    It is also noteworthy that there is a dramatic
asymmetry in terms of responses to increases in
risk, as opposed to decreases. Whereas the
willingness to pay amounts for decreases in risks
summarized in Table 5-2 were fairly modest, when
respondents were told that the risk would
increase, there were widespread alarmist
reactions. Risk increases of the same order
of magnitude as the risk decreases--5/10,000--led
all respondents to indicate that they would not
purchase a product at all. When the study design
was changed to permit risk increases of 1/10,000
the majority of respondents continued to indicate
that they would not purchase a product at any
price. In cases where they did express a
willingness to purchase and accept a price
reduction for that risk, then their rate of
tradeoff greatly exceeded their tradeoff rate for
risk decreases. What this phenomenon indicates
is that there is an important "reference risk"

Table 5-2

Marginal Valuations of Reducing Both
Risks by $/10,000

Incremental Willingness to Pay (dollars/bottle)

Starting Risk (injuries/10,000 bottles)	Inhalation- Skin Poisoning	Inhalation- Child Poisoning	Gassing Eyeburn	Gassing- Child Poisoning
15	1.04	1.84	.65	.99
10	.34	.54	.19	.24
5	2.41	5.71	.83	.99

effect as individuals display substantial
reluctance to accept any increase in the risk
above the level that currently is posed by the
product. Thus, when they are told that the
product has become riskier and are given
information regarding the magnitude of the
risk increase, they tend to over-assess the risk
increase associated with this information.

   5.   Use of on-product labels leads consumers
        to conclude that the product poses a
        higher risk.

   Perhaps the most neglected feature of a hazard
warning is that the very act of placing a warning
on a product is to designate it as being in a
risky class of products. In effect, what we are
doing is stamping some products as being high risk
and other products as not being of high risk when
we make distinctions as to which products merit
warnings and which do not. Thus, much of the risk

information conveyed by the label stems from the
fact that there is a hazard warning in place
rather than the specific content of the warning
itself.

A striking illustration of this result occurred
when I presented a series of chemical warning
labels to several audiences, including one class
at Harvard Law School and a National Bureau of
Economic Research Conference. In each case I
polled the audience regarding the risk that they
believe they would face on a job in which they
used the chemical "sodium bicarbonate." The
hazard warning gave information regarding
appropriate precautions to take with respect to
this chemical, such as cleaning it up after a
spill. Otherwise, the format structure of the
hazard warning label was similar to that of
hazard warnings for risky products except that the
labeling included no specific information
indicating the risk; nor did it include any human
hazard signal words, such as "danger." I then
polled the audience with respect to the risk that
they believed they would face if they had to work
with this chemical as part of their job, and the
great majority of respondents believed that
working with the chemical sodium bicarbonate would
be an above average risk job in the chemical
industry. When informed that this product was in
fact simply household baking soda, the almost
universal response was that this product should
not have been labeled if in fact it was not truly
risky. Although other groups of respondents with
more experience in the kitchen may be able to
make a more knowledgeable assessment of a sodium
bicarbonate warning, the essential point of this
example is not that individuals were unfamiliar
with household products, but rather that in
situations in which they did not know the
implications of a particular product, a warning
may have a substantial effect on their risk
perceptions even if we do not provide any specific

risk information as part of the label.

6.   Ill-conceived warnings programs are
     damaging to other warnings efforts.

This principle is simply a generalization of
the fourth and fifth principles to the entire
warning context. For the same types of reasons
that we do not wish to clutter an individual
label, we also do not wish to clutter the entire
set of risk communication messages that an
individual receives. Thus, we want to reserve
hazard warnings for the true risks so that
individuals can be selective in the information
that they acquire about the hazards.

The informational content of labels, which was
the essential theme of the fifth guideline given
above, will also be jeopardized to the extent that
we use labels indiscriminately. If everything in
society is labeled, in effect nothing will be
labeled since all products will be treated
symmetrically. What we want to do is reserve
labeling as a means for designating higher risk
products and in doing so we should be selective in
the manner in which we use the labeling mechanism.

The six principles given above do not provide
precise guidelines for writing the text of
particular labels, but they do provide an overview
of the principles that should be kept in mind
when approaching a hazard communication problem.
They also provide the conceptual backdrop for
assessing which institution is best equipped to
handle the hazard communication tasks. Designing
a hazard warning program is a non-trivial task
that must be done systematically across products,
and ideally we would want to select institutions
that could accomplish this task in a uniform and
effective manner. In this next section we will
address these institutional issues in greater
detail.

Institutional Context of Hazards Warning Programs

Before considering the performance of
particular hazard warnings efforts, it is helpful
to provide a brief review of the different
institutions that we could utilize to develop
society's hazard warnings efforts. The natural
starting point for any such discussion is to ask
why we do not let private markets assume this
function. The incentive to provide risk
information associated with products will not be
completely non-existent, but will be inadequate
for two reasons. First, information by nature
tends to be a public good. To the extent that
firms are assuming the task of educating the
public with respect to more general risks, they
will not undertake the needed effort to a degree
that is socially optimal. Second, if these firms
are providing information that is damaging to the
attractiveness of their products, they will not
have an economic incentive to do so. Thus, if
individuals are unaware of a risk of a product
there is an economic disincentive on the part of
the manufacturer to call these risks to consumers'
attention, particularly given the tendency of
individuals to respond in an alarmist manner to
risks associated with products.
Despite these limitations, private incentives
for risk communication are not completely
non-existent. If a firm develops a reputation for
putting products on the market and not fully
informing consumers, leading to a record of
substantial accidents, there will be an adverse
consumer response to the product. Appropriate
precautionary instruction can be viewed as
one of the product attributes that consumers are
purchasing. When there are apparent risks of the
product and consumers are aware that they are not
being given the information needed to use the
product safely, one would expect there to be a
decrease in the attractiveness of the product to

consumers.

The ideal mechanism for establishing a risk
communication system is through a national effort
administered by a Federal regulatory agency.
National warnings efforts have an advantage in
that they can establish a uniform risk vocabulary.
The warning format as well as the severity
associated with different forms of warning
language ideally should be controlled to be
uniform across the product, and this can best be
accomplished through a national regulatory policy.

Perhaps the most striking example of a
successful warning program is the pharmaceutical
warning effort administered by the Food and Drug
Administration. Package inserts for prescription
drugs are required to include a variety of forms
of risk information as well as information
regarding proper usage of the product. The
structure of the information is tightly controlled
by the FDA, and there is detailed examination of
the character of the warning provided to ensure
that it is consistent with the severity of
warnings given across products. Thus, both the
structure and the content of the warning have been
normalized in a manner that can readily
communicate to the recipient group (physicians)
the properties of the product. Although not all
Federal warning efforts are ideal, from an
institutional standpoint a Federal regulatory
approach does have the greatest potential for
success.

Another form of Federal intervention could be
through the U.S. Congress, which is responsible
for the warning labels for cigarettes, saccharin,
and the proposed alcohol beverage warnings.
Whereas the FDA primarily uses a team of
pharmacologists and other medical experts to
design appropriate warning language for a
prescription drug, congressional efforts
are dictated largely by the work of lawyers. This
professional orientation is not ideal since the

focus is not so much on risk communication but on developing language that will solve an immediate political problem. As I will indicate in the fourth section in my discussion of the alcoholic beverage warning, the proposed warning language stems more from the influence of special interest groups lobbying for particular forms of warnings than it does from any sound consideration of a proper hazard communications system.

A fourth alternative is to have the regulation undertaken by the states rather than by a branch of the Federal Government. The difficulty with state regulation of hazard warnings efforts is that many products are distributed nationally so that state-by state regulation is infeasible. Such warnings would have to be applied to products at the warehouse. More generally, if we have a warning system that does not adopt a uniform national vocabulary we run the danger of having a distorted mix of messages reaching consumers. The perils of state regulation will be illustrated by the case study of the California food cancer risk regulation, which is the subject of the fifth section.

A final alternative is to rely upon the courts to design hazard warnings. In terms of timing, courts act after the fact so that it is only after injuries have occurred that courts will address the hazard warning issue. Moreover, the hazard warnings policy option tends to be discussed only in situations where there is no other strong basis for establishing fault on the part of the product producer. Thus, in situations where plaintiffs cannot otherwise prove negligence or liability on the part of the producer, it is often shown that the warning is inadequate and as a result there is a design defect in terms of the character of the warning accompanying the product. Situations in which other liability doctrines are operative or in which there are no product accidents that are litigated consequently will not be considered by the courts.

Moreover, in situations where the courts are considering the warnings there is a danger that the procedure will be very myopic. Expert witnesses typically testify that if only there had been a prominent warning for the particular accident in question then it never would have occurred. Considering risks on a piecemeal basis such as this is not appropriate, however. Our task is not to develop a hazard warning for a particular risk, but rather to develop a sound hazard communication system for the whole cluster of risks involved with a particular product. Although a particular issue may loom large in a specific court case, it may not be of substantial consequence when considered within the entire context of all the risks posed by a product.

One highly litigated class of risk concerns that exemplifies this phenomenon is the tipover risk associated with forklift trucks. It has often been suggested that if firms had a more prominent warning on the truck regarding the tipover hazard, then these accidents would not have occurred. More careful examination of the training manuals accompanying these trucks indicates that there are roughly 30 to 40 major sources of risk that can lead to fatalities, so that if we were to carry this warnings approach to the extreme then we would have a product that was, in effect, covered with labels.

In lieu of labels, firms could adopt other forms of risk communication that are more appropriate to the particular context, which in the case of lift trucks has been done in terms of training manuals, training video tapes, as well as formal training programs for lift truck operators. Despite these efforts, courts have not displayed as much of a willingness to consider the entire set of hazard communication activities as well as the need for balance in a hazard communication system since the court's perspective tends to be distorted by the risk at hand.

More generally, one difficulty with court decisions is that they often lead to anticipatory labeling actions on the part of firms in an effort to protect themselves against prospective liability rather than to truly communicate the risks to consumers. The existing warnings for pesticide products are a case in point, as the warnings are, in effect, detailed booklets that are unlikely to be read and, if read, would not be understood. These warnings nevertheless do provide printed documentation of the product risks and appropriate use so that in the event of a court case the defendant will have concrete evidence to point to as evidence of an appropriate hazard warnings program. If anything, the net effect of court actions has been deleterious rather than helpful in promoting a national warnings vocabulary and a sound hazard communication system across all products.

Analysis of Proposed Alcohol Beverage Warnings[11]

A particularly prominent case study of hazard warnings is the proposed 1988 Senate bill (S.2047) that would mandate on-product labels for alcoholic beverages. This effort is of interest for two reasons. First, consideration of the content of the warning is particularly instructive since it illustrates the potential pitfalls that can be encountered if one does not heed the six principles for the development of a sound hazard warnings policy that were outlined in the second section of the chapter. In addition, the structure of the warnings that have been proposed illustrates the potentially deleterious influence of special interests groups as, in effect, the warnings language has been adopted to maximize this political appeal rather than to convey new information that might be helpful in improving decisions.

Table 5-3 summarizes the proposed warning
language, which consists of five specific warnings
to appear on alcoholic beverages in a rotating
fashion. Although modifications of this
warning language have since been proposed, this
set of warnings is nevertheless of interest since
it reflects the general character of the entire
warnings effort in the alcohol area. States such
as Massachusetts, for example, are considering
warnings efforts of this type.

What is particularly noteworthy about the
warnings is that each of the warnings components
has its own particular constituency. Indeed, the
congressional hearings that were held on this
issue included a variety of special interest
groups, each of which testified on behalf of its
particular warning as being an important component
of the hazard communication system.[12]

One group of participants is the medical
community. A variety of medical groups have
endorsed the general principle of hazard warnings
for alcohol, and researchers on fetal alcohol
syndrome were present to support the first warning
pertaining to the pregnancy risks of alcohol.[13]
There was, however, no specific advocacy by the
medical community of the particular language used
in the other warnings appearing in the group in
Table 5-3.

A second constituency for hazard warnings
consists of religious groups that oppose the use
of alcohol. These views may have influenced in
part the position taken by Senator Strom Thurmond,
who represents South Carolina. Coverage in the
Washington Post on the day of the hearing
indicated that some observers believed that
individuals with prohibitionist leanings were
playing an important role in advocating the
legislation.[14]

A third constituency was the set of consumer
groups that opposed drunken driving. Warning no.
2 is directed at their interests.

Table 5-3

Proposed Alcohol Beverage Warning

---

(1) WARNING: THE SURGEON GENERAL HAS DETERMINED THAT THE CONSUMPTION OF THIS PRODUCT, WHICH CONTAINS ALCOHOL, DURING PREGNANCY CAN CAUSE MENTAL RETARDATION AND OTHER BIRTH DEFECTS.

(2) WARNING: DRINKING THIS PRODUCT, WHICH CONTAINS ALCOHOL, IMPAIRS YOUR ABILITY TO DRIVE A CAR OR OPERATE MACHINERY.

(3) WARNING: THIS PRODUCT CONTAINS ALCOHOL AND IS PARTICULARLY HAZARDOUS IN COMBINATION WITH SOME DRUGS.

(4) WARNING: THE CONSUMPTION OF THIS PRODUCT, WHICH CONTAINS ALCOHOL, CAN INCREASE THE RISK OF DEVELOPING HYPERTENSION, LIVER DISEASE, AND CANCER.

(5) WARNING: ALCOHOL IS A DRUG AND MAY BE ADDICTIVE.

Finally, a fourth constituency consists of those opposing alcoholism. This group supported the entire set of warnings, but particularly warning no. 5.

The result has been a politically determined grab bag of warnings for a very large variety of potential risks associated with the use of alcohol, which is one of the most widely consumed and well understood products in the United States. It is helpful to consider each of the warnings to assess whether or not they are potentially desirable. The most useful framework for doing so is to follow the six principles that were established in the second section.

The first principle is that a hazard warning system should convey new information to the individuals receiving the warning. Warning no. 2 (which indicates that drinking can impair one's driving ability) and warning no. 5 (which in

effect indicates that too much drinking can make
one an alcoholic) do not provide new knowledge to
consumers and as a consequence would not be
effective warnings. The health risk warning no. 4
also overlaps with a the variety of recent public
information efforts, and it is unclear what this
warning would add to existing public knowledge.

At present, alcohol risks are among the most
highly publicized and well known risks in our
society. When Americans are asked to cite major
problems facing our nation, eighty one percent
list alcohol abuse as a major national problem,
and only two percent of all respondents do not
view it as a national problem.[15]

The drunken driving risks covered by warning
no. 2 have long been a target of public education
campaigns. The risks of driving and drinking are
well known, obvious, and receive substantial
publicity. Newspaper coverage of these risks has
increased by a factor of more than thirty (Nexis
count of AP stories) in the past decade. This
press coverage has included the health risks
captured in warning no. 4 as well. The number
of AP articles per year on fitness and alcohol,
diet and alcohol, or alcohol abuse has increased
more than ten-fold in the past decade. The effect
of these efforts has been so great that more
teenagers now tend to view alcohol as a greater
risk than cigarette smoking.[16] More to the point
than these factual quiz questions is that the
risks and dangers of alcoholism are universally
understood. What will warning no. 5 add to this
knowledge? Do we want people to believe that
"moderate" heroin use carries no more risk than
moderate alcohol use?

Even warning no. 1 for alcohol risks to
pregnant women may have little informational
content. Although many people cannot define
"fetal alcohol syndrome," nitpicking over medical
definitions is not the issue. There is already a
widespread belief that drinking can be harmful to

a fetus. A 1985 Gallup Poll indicated that 90% of
the population agree strongly or somewhat that
"the use of alcohol by pregnant women can cause
birth defects."[17] This response reflects
substantial awareness of the risks, particularly
given the wording of the question. If this survey
had dealt with alcohol abuse rather than including
moderate drinking as well, no doubt a greater
fraction of the population would have expressed
awareness. In addition, over three-fourths of all
women of childbearing age list alcohol as a
substance they should avoid.[18] Based on my past
experience with running open-ended memory recall
studies such as this, I view this result as a very
striking response given the unprompted nature of
the survey.

Although there is clearly a potential need for
continued media coverage and public education
regarding the diverse risks posed by misuse of
alcohol, the series of one sentence statements
regarding these risks that appears in the proposed
warning language offers little by way of new
information that will augment the knowledge that
individuals already have. Rather, the warnings are
more in the form of reminders and attempted
persuasion, which is a warnings mode that has not
been shown to be effective.

The second guideline articulated in the second
section is that we should provide both risk and
precaution information as part of the hazard warning. As the review of the warnings in Table 5-3
indicates, these warnings consist merely of risks
that are brought to consumers' attention, but
there is generally no discussion of precautions.
In effect, one could most likely characterize
these warnings as being in the form: "Don't buy
this product since..." Such a warning policy is
not completely non-informative, but I do not
believe it is credible. The warnings are overly
broad and seem to indicate that any quantity

of the product whatsoever is harmful, whereas the main societal concern is with abuse, not use.

Such indiscriminating warnings do not convey accurate information. Although pregnant women are urged not to drink at all because the safe level of consumption has not been determined, moderate drinking in the general population has not been associated with the risks to be communicated by the proposed labels. Indeed, the recent Surgeon General's Report on Nutrition and Health concludes "consumption of one to two drinks per day has not been associated with disease among healthy male and non-pregnant female adults."[19] The risks related to alcohol accelerate at high alcohol consumption levels, and the warnings do not make this clear. Thus, the warnings convey inadequate information that will either misinform consumers or fail to be credible.

The warning with respect to combining alcohol and drugs seems to be particularly inappropriate. Alerting consumers to a general link does not enable them to make the distinction with respect to specific adverse interactions. Combining alcohol with barbiturates poses a quite different risk than combining alcohol with aspirin. A more sensible approach, which we now have, is to provide warnings for the drugs that pose particularly large risks when associated with alcohol. In addition, physicians bear responsibility for instructing patients in the proper use of products that they prescribe, and it is these prescription drugs that pose the greatest interactive danger. The pharmaceutical industry and the medical profession should not be permitted to shift their responsibilities to an all-purpose warning that is not well designed for enabling consumers to make decisions on specific drugs.

The third guideline is that on-product labels are most effective only for limited information transfer. Labels are most useful as a warning device in situations in which reading the label is

an essential part of using the product. Consumers
need not read the beer, wine, or liquor warning in
order to drink the product. In many cases, they
do not even see the container during their use of
the product.

In situations in which one wishes to convey a
fairly complex message, a label is not the best
alternative. I would characterize S. 2047
warnings 1,3, and 4 as being complex. Ideally,
one would like to tell individuals much more than
the simple statements indicated, such as linking
alcohol to birth defects and cancer. One might
want to educate people regarding the amount of
alcohol that is involved in such causal links, the
duration and frequency of such risk exposures and
how they affect the risks, etc. Such information
is too lengthy and complex to be suitable for a
short alcohol beverage label.

More generally, it would seem that there are
other information transfer mechanisms that are
more appropriate for conveying this message. In
the case of the warning to pregnant women,
physicians can provide a much more capable and
credible mechanism for conveying the warning. In
the case of the broader health risks of alcohol,
longer treatments of the issue in the media would
be much more effective, as would education
programs in our schools. Health and welfare
agencies at both the state and federal level can
contribute to this discussion, and some alcohol
producers have done so as well. Adverse
combinations of alcohol and drugs should be
handled through physician advice and the warning
labels on the drugs for which there are
potentially dangerous interactions. The
dissemination of information is important, but
labels on alcohol are not the most appropriate
means for accomplishing this task.

The fourth concern is that labeling alcohol as
being risky is overly simplistic. Introduction of
an alcohol warnings label system, particularly one

that places alcohol in the same class as addictive
drugs such as heroin, would convey to consumers
that alcoholic beverages pose a very high risk to
all the consumers of the product, irrespective of
its use. The main difficulty with this warning is
that it fails to indicate that the main risk
stems from abuse of the product not from use so
that the product is not always risky. Except for
the qualifiers regarding risks to pregnant women
and drug interaction, the warnings listed in
Table 5-3 are indiscriminate in terms of their
coverage.

The specific form of warnings that was
adopted--a rotating warnings policy--runs counter
to the general principle of providing a
comprehensive warning message. The support for
the rotation policies stems largely from the
Madison Avenue approach to advertising for which
the advertising message is altered to avoid
boredom by consumers. Our intent, however, is to
convey risks in a systematic manner, not to
capture the imagination of a supposedly irrational
consumer who is looking for the hazard warning
equivalent of a catchy product slogan. To date,
there is no evidence in the literature that
supports the fragmentation of warnings policies in
this manner.

The main deficiency of the warnings system
developed by Congress is that the objective of
informing consumers and developing a sound hazard
communication system has not been advanced.
Rather than focusing on new information regarding
risks and precautions that conveys in a concise
manner the information needed by consumers to make
sound decisions, what we have instead is a diverse
set of warnings about risks, with no indication
regarding the precautions and also no refined
information indicating the linkage of these risks
to the abuse of alcohol. In some cases, the basic
warning message is so well known that any hazard
communication effort would seem to demand a

much more subtle and detailed approach than can be afforded through the use of labels. For the risks posed to pregnant women, a more appropriate and effective means for conveying information beyond what women already know about these hazards, which is a great deal, would be to rely on the medical community and physicians rather than a one sentence statement on a warning label. In a situation in which the warning must be compressed into a single sentence, one runs the danger of having an inaccurate warning, which could threaten the credibility of the entire warnings effort. In particular, in the case of fetal alcohol syndrome risks, there is no evidence that links these risks to alcohol use of under two drinks per day, as the Surgeon General simply advises women to avoid use at such low levels so that they can err on the side of conservatism given the uncertainty of our scientific knowledge. A more appropriate risk information program would be to convey the entire richness of the Surgeon General's message rather than trying to distill it into a more dictatorial form that at present does not have scientific support. A major danger for any risk communication effort is that we should not jeopardize its credibility since doing so may lead individuals to dismiss other warnings now and in the future.

Food Cancer Warnings

The principles for developing a sound warning system can also be illustrated by examining what may be the most far-reaching warnings effort in the 1980s. In 1986, California voters passed a referendum known as Proposition 65, which was entitled the Safe Drinking Water and Toxic Enforcement Act of 1986. Although this statute has a number of major policy ramifications, including job and environmental warnings requirements, the focus of my discussion will be

on the food cancer warning requirements. In
particular, by February 1988 all food products
containing chemicals that pose significant risks
of cancer had to be accompanied by a warning that
would be effective in communicating these risks.
Although most products were granted a temporary
exemption while the risks were being assessed,
others such as tobacco and alcoholic beverages
have been actively involved in the warnings
controversy and litigation efforts.

Overall, the idea of instituting a food cancer
warning policy is long overdue. In principle a
warnings policy is a good idea. Federal
regulatory policies have not and should not
eliminate all cancer risks, however small they
might be. For those risks that remain after
Federal regulation, individuals may have quite
different attitudes toward their willingness to
bear the risks and toward their commitment to
particular products in view of these risks. By
providing individuals with risk information so
that they can make decisions that reflect their
preferences, a hazard warnings policy can take
advantage of the ability of market forces to
establish an efficient match-up between
individuals and the risks they face.

To reap these benefits, however, a warnings
policy must provide risk information in a manner
that will enable consumers to make these risk
distinctions. Unfortunately, the implementation
of the California policy will not provide either
accurate information or sufficiently refined
information to foster more informed decisions.
The basic difficulty with the California
initiative is that it failed to reflect an
understanding of how individuals process risk
information and how the policy should be designed
to foster improved risk-averting decisions. The
main missing ingredient has been a lack of
concern with individuals' decision processes.
Since a right-to-know policy will only be

effective if it engages individual actions in the desired manner, this was a critical oversight.

The Case for Food Cancer Warnings

The existing panoply of governmental regulations eliminates the most severe hazards in our food chain. Many nonzero risks will remain since some risks cannot be reduced at all (e.g., the estragole in basil), and others may be quite costly to eliminate so that it is not desirable to do so (e.g., chloroform in tap water). The consumer outcry after the attempt to ban saccharin is perhaps the most notable recent example of a desire to have certain products available even though they may not be risk-free.

In the absence of a hazard warnings policy, society essentially has two options. Either we could ban a particular product altogether, or we could permit it to be sold with no policy restrictions whatsoever. Having such a limited and extreme set of policy choices may lead to compromises in policy stringency that are undesirable, such as banning substances posing minimal risks or taking no action whatsoever against product risks that are not serious enough to warrant a ban. The absence of a diversity of policy options will also lead to a failure to reflect differences in consumer preferences with respect to such risks.

Food cancer warning policies can potentially address these risks falling in the intermediate range by providing information to consumers so that individuals who wish to avoid cancer risks can do so. At present, such information is not readily accessible. It is easy for consumers to monitor whether produce is fresh or has been bruised, but whether this produce has also been drenched in pesticides cannot be ascertained upon inspection at the grocery store. Indeed, such produce may look particularly healthy. Similarly, even for products with a listing of

chemical ingredients, such information is often
not helpful unless one has chosen to adopt an
overly conservative "no additives" diet. Not
all chemicals are carcinogenic, and many
carcinogens occur naturally or within the course
of food storage and processing so that the "no
additives" approach will rule out many harmless
substances and include many naturally occurring
carcinogens. The policy objective is simple.
What we need is a more targeted form of
information that will enable consumers to make
meaningful distinctions with respect to cancer
risks.

We can expect an effective food cancer warning
policy to influence the behavior of some, but not
necessarily all consumers. Indeed, if it were our
objective to eliminate consumption of a product
then we should not be relying on a hazard warning
program. Rather, we should be pursuing an attempt
to ban the product altogether. The objective for
food cancer warnings should not necessarily be to
discourage consumption of these products. For
much the same reason, the Surgeon General's
objective of a "smoke-free society" is misguided.
Rather, the objective should be informed consumer
choice. Individuals should be given sufficient
risk information so that they can make
meaningful cancer risk decisions.

This objective does not presuppose fully
rational behavior on the part of consumers. Risky
choices impose notoriously difficult demands on
individual rationality. The existence of
these departures from rationality does not doom
informational policies to failure, but they do
suggest a need or taking these characteristics of
individual decision making into account when
designing the warnings program. For example, it
is not generally effective to tell people that a
product poses a specific cancer risk such as
.00001. Through appropriate design of the content
and format of the warning, we can, however, convey

a comparable risk message that will lead to the desired behavior. The existence of shortcomings in individual decision making does not imply that hazard warnings efforts are doomed to failure, but it does suggest that the government should design hazard warnings efforts taking individuals' cognitive limitations into account.

Perhaps the major achievement of Proposition 65 is that it put the food cancer warning policy issue on the national risk regulation agenda. The specific features of the regulation as it has been implemented are less laudable.

The basic mission of Proposition 65 in the food cancer area is to warn consumers of all risks judged to be "significant." Determination of significance involves substantial scientific input, in particular with respect to determining levels of carcinogenicity of different substances. Unfortunately, the scientific basis for the Proposition 65 warnings policy is basically dishonest. The policy follows the usual "conservatism" practices that are widely used in the federal government by focusing on results for the most sensitive animal species, focusing on the upper end of the 95% confidence interval for the risk rather than the mean estimate of the risk, reliance on a linear does-response relationships, and similar conservatism biases. The net effect of these practices is to overstate the risks by an uncertain magnitude rather than to provide unbiased estimates of the true risk posed to consumers.

Such "conservatism" is inappropriate within the context of an informational policy. The basic objective of an information program is to provide accurate knowledge to consumers. If we base these policies on fundamentally distorted scientific evidence, with biases that may vary greatly from substance to substance, then we run the risk of jeopardizing the credibility of such programs as well as of misleading consumers regarding the true risks that are posed.

Even if we were to base policies on unbiased risk assessments, we must then select what particular level of risk is "significant." Determination of significance within the context of an information program is essentially a policy question rather than a scientific question. The number of digits attached to a risk is not a true test of significance. What we really want to know is whether these risks will be of sufficient magnitude that consumers should take them into account when making their decisions. Thus, significance must be defined within an operational context based on its effect on informed decisions rather than viewed as an abstract notion linked to the number of zeros in the risk probability statistic.

A decision-oriented approach to significance is the following. The California regulation requires warnings for all products posing a "significant" lifetime risk, where a lifetime is defined to be 70 years. If a consumer were to purchase a product weekly for each of those 70 years, and if this consumer had an attitude toward risk similar to that of the typical worker when facing risks on the job (e.g., an implicit value per statistical life lost of $4,000,000-$5,000,000), then a lifetime risk of 1/100,000 would alter his weekly purchase decisions for the product by under a penny. Thus, one might view the lifetime risk of the product of 1/100,000 as being a de minimis risk level that can serve as a threshold for all risk policies. It is the lowest risk that conceivably might make a difference economically, which is an essential ingredient for the program to have any effect. After originally focusing on a 1/1,000,000 threshold, California selected the 1/100,000 threshold level, but in their case this threshold is the significant risk threshold rather than a de minimis threshold.

It is instructive to compare this risk

threshold with risks regulated by the government.
The 1/100,000 risk in a lifetime threshold is at
the low end of risks regulated by the Federal
government. Almost all risks that have been
regulated are significantly greater, such as the
cancer risks facing asbestos workers and
individuals exposed to arsenic emissions in
the environment. Indeed, the only smaller
lifetime risks among recently proposed major
Federal regulations are those covered by
proposed EPA land disposal requirements and FAA
airplane safety regulations, if one assumes that
people fly an average of only once per year.[20]
Similarly, lifetime cancer risks from saccharin
or cigarette smoking are believed to be several
orders of magnitude greater than the Proposition
65 cut off. In short, a lifetime risk of
1/100,000, which translates into an annual risk
of 1/7,000,000, is very low indeed. The risk
threshold for a warnings policy should be
relatively low since direct controls and bans are
used for more substantial hazards. The small
nature of the risk is not necessarily reason for
inaction, but it does suggest that whatever policy
we do pursue should be commensurate with the risk
level.

The implications of Proposition 65 are still
not fully apparent since California is still in
the process of designating the chemicals that
merit consideration when determining significant
risk levels. A prominent recent action was the
addition of alcohol to the list of potential
carcinogens. Based on scientific evidence on
potential carcinogenicity, an effective food
cancer warning policy would include, among others,
the following products: natural root beer,
mushrooms, basil, brown mustard, and bacon.
California's exemption of "naturally occurring"
carcinogens, such as those present in fish,
reduces the scope of Proposition 65's coverage and
also diminishes its informational value in making

across-product comparisons.

Once a product has passed this threshold, consumers must be given a warning regarding the risks posed by the product. It is in this area that the California policymakers are perhaps most remiss. They appear to have interpreted their objective of providing effective warnings as tantamount to providing the strongest warning possible. Instead, they should have selected warnings that convey the risk most accurately. Thus, they have confused impact with effectiveness.

The wording that they have chosen parallels quite closely the recent hazard warnings for cigarettes:

> WARNING: This Product Contains a
> Chemical Known to the State
> of California to Cause Cancer.

This is a strong warning indeed that states a well-defined link to cancer in a clear and concise manner. Such a warning seems particularly inappropriate given the low risks involved. In addition, any such warning will be filtered by the limited cognitive capabilities of individuals. Since individuals tend to overestimate low probability risks that are called to their attention, any such warning runs the risk of excessive alarm.

Although there are a variety of studies in the literature that enable one to make judgments on such issues, a more reliable basis for assessing the implications of the warning is to test its actual effect on consumers. This is particularly important since there is a broad range of conceivable effects that the warning might have. Although we can be confident that the warning appears to be excessive, we do not know specifically how much the warning errs in terms of exaggerations in the implied risk level.

To pin this implied risk level down more precisely, I undertook a small scale study with 99 participants in a continuing education program held at Northwestern University. These adult students were told that their breakfast cereal had a hazard warning on it. The experimental manipulations included a warning identical to the California Proposition 65 warning, except that I replaced "California" with "Illinois" in the warning language. Consumers were then asked a series of questions with respect to the risk. Table 5-4 reports a ranking of this particular warning with respect to other warning wordings, where these results are based on a series of pairwise warning comparisons. The first warning wording listed in Table 5-4 is the present warning for saccharin products. The second warning wording is a variant of the 1969 cigarette warning, and the third warning is the 1965 cigarette warning.

Table 5-4

Comparisons of California Warning with Other Wordings

	Fraction Who Regard as Less Risky	Fraction Who Regard as Equally Risky	Fraction Who Regard as More Risky
1. Use of this product may be hazardous to your health. This product contains a chemical that has been determined to cause cancer in laboratory animals.	.56	.18	.26
2. Warning: The State of Illinois has determined that this product is dangerous to your health.	.36	.48	.16
3. Caution: Use of this product may be hazardous to your health.	.14	.69	.17

Consider first the comparison with the
saccharin warning. The majority of consumers
regarded the saccharin warning as implying a lower
risk than the cereal that included the
Proposition 65 warning, and only one-fourth of the
respondents viewed the saccharin warning as being
riskier. The result is particularly striking
since the same kinds of scientific studies
that will generate the 1/100,000 risk threshold
for products covered by Proposition 65 have led to
a lifetime risk estimate of 1/2500 for saccharin.
The saccharin risks are consequently much more
substantial, but are covered with a warning that
is viewed as less stringent.

The cigarette warnings are viewed as comparable
to the Proposition 65 warnings by a substantial
portion of the consumers. Thus, Proposition 65
will be providing warnings that have roughly the
same impact as those placed on cigarettes, which
the Surgeon General claims pose a lifetime cancer
risk that is much greater.

The difficulty is that consumers will be using
these reference points for products that have
warnings already to assess where the products
covered by the Proposition 65 warning lie in this
consumer product risk continuum. If the only
information we give consumers is a warning that
pegs the product at the high end of the risk
range, then we have not provided them with
information, but have instead led to excessive
alarm.

A second test that I utilize to assess
consumers' response to the warnings is to ask them
to rate the risks associated with the Proposition
65 warning. Consumers had to pick a particular
risk range for the product, where the three risk
ranges are summarized in Table 5-5. The first
risk range was from zero risk to the risk posed by
one twelve ounce cola containing saccharin. The
second risk range was from one saccharin cola to
one pack of cigarettes, and the third risk range

Table 5-5

Risk Assessment for Proposition 65 Warning

	Risk Range	Fraction Who Put Product in Range	Score within Range on a 10 pt. Scale
1.	Zero Risk - 1 12 oz. Saccharin Cola	.21	4.86
2.	1 Saccharin Cola - 1 Pack of Cigarettes	.44	4.27
3.	1 Pack of Cigarettes - 5 Packs of Cigarettes	.35	2.25

was from one pack of cigarettes to five packs of cigarettes.

About 1/5 of the consumers rated the risk as being midway between zero and that posed by one twelve ounce soft drink containing saccharin. Forty-four percent of the consumers rated the risk as being midway between one saccharin cola and one pack of cigarettes, and 35% of the consumers rated the risk as being between one and five packs of cigarettes, with an average risk assessment in this group of about two packs of cigarettes per day. The overall average for these responses is that even if we view the risk of saccharin colas as being zero, consumers view products containing the Proposition 65 warning as posing the same risk as smoking .58 packs of cigarettes per day.

As a third test of the effect of the warning, I then asked the consumers how many of 11,000,000 Illinois residents would be likely to die from a product bearing a Proposition 65 warning if they were to consume it daily throughout their lives. The average response was that 1,316,729 consumers would die, or that the lifetime risk of cancer was

.12. This response is roughly 10,000 times
greater than what the Proposition 65 risk
threshold would be even if there were no
conservatism used in establishing the underlying
scientific basis for the regulation. It is also
noteworthy that these results imply that consumers
estimated the lifetime cancer risk of a daily pack
of cigarettes as being .21, which implies a
lifetime risk for the typical smoker of 0.33. The
cigarette risk assessment value greatly exceeds
current estimates of the hazards posed by cigarettes. These results are not surprising given
the substantial literature documenting individual over-assessment of low probability events.

The rather striking nature of these alarmist
responses to the Proposition 65 warning suggests
the need for a more thoughtful and careful
approach toward warning design. We cannot simply
replicate hazard warnings from other contexts and
hope that they will convey what might be quite
different risk levels. In addition it is
irresponsible from a policy standpoint to launch a
major warnings initiative without doing detailed
pretesting to ascertain that the information we
are providing will lead to more informed
decisions.

How we provide the information is also of
substantial consequence. In particular, risks
will not be communicated to consumers if they do
not receive the information. Ideally, one would
like to have a warnings mode that provided
information to consumers in a systematic fashion
to enable them to make their purchase and
consumption decisions.

What we have instead is an open-ended grab bag
of options from which firms are permitted to
choose. On-product labels are one possibility,
but this is an unattractive option for producers
who will find it difficult to place separate
labels on products targeted for the California
market. A second option is the use of shelf

labels and in-store displays, but this approach
shifts the nuisance and burdens associated with
the warnings to grocery manufacturers, who not
unexpectedly have opposed this means of
compliance. Alcoholic beverage warnings are,
however, handled through such a display since the
commonality of the risks across products makes
such a collective warning feasible. Other modes
of compliance include the use of cash register
receipts containing hazard warning information as
well as the use of a toll-free telephone number,
which has been a very popular compliance mode.
The toll free number faces a court challenge by
environmentalists, who refer to this policy option
as 1-800-BALONEY.

What is clear is that the variety of different
modes of compliance makes it difficult for
consumers to ascertain how they should go about
getting the warning information. The nature of
the warning in terms of the manner it is
communicated may differ from product to product,
imposing substantial information acquisition
costs. In this particular policy context, choice
and flexibility in terms of the mode of compliance
is not desirable. Rather, we want a system that
promotes commonality in approach and warning
format both to ensure comparability and to improve
the ease with which consumers can acquire the
needed information. The 800 number approach that
has been adopted on a widespread basis satisfies
this consistency requirement.

Moreover, the mode of the warning must be
commensurate with the risk. The very act of
requiring an on-product label has informational
content. Society has designated this product as
being at the high end of the risk range. We
should reserve the use of such warnings for
situations in which the risks are truly
consequential. Below I outline a policy proposal
that incorporates a differential warnings approach
so that the hazard warning can be altered

depending on the severity of the risk.

California Proposition 65 has played a constructive role in highlighting the need for a food cancer warning policy. However, this policy should be Federal rather than state. Because of the division of Federal authority over food-related products (i.e., the U.S. Department of the Treasury has responsibility for alcohol, the U.S. Department of Agriculture has responsibility for meat, the Food and Drug Administration (FDA) has responsibility for other food products, and the Environmental Protection Agency (EPA) has responsibility for drinking water), there is a need for a coordinated rulemaking effort by these agencies. These issues would not be entirely new to the agencies' agendas. EPA, for example, has elaborate pesticide label requirements and has been considering drinking water warnings in recent years.

The usual arguments for state rather than Federal regulation is that such policies can reflect differences in preferences across states. Consumers in California may be more concerned with carcinogens than those in Kentucky. With an informational policy, however, there is no requirement that individuals take a particular course of action. Rather, we are only ensuring that they have the information that is required to make a knowledgeable risk-averting decision. If avoiding cancer risks is not highly valued, they need not alter their consumption pattern.

Any food warning effort should treat cancer risks from all sources. The California exemptions for naturally occurring carcinogens, additives regulated by the FDA, and meat subject to Federal regulation should be eliminated. The warnings policy should inform consumers of cancer risks from all sources so that meaningful comparisons across products can be made in assessing the overall degree of riskiness, from whatever cause.

Perhaps the most important component of any such policy should be to make more distinctions in terms of the level of risk conveyed. The on-off designation of products as being carcinogenic is too simplistic. In addition, if we were to include very low risks in any hazard warning effort, then we should not be using on-product labels, which should be reserved for the truly serious risks posed in our society.

As a result, I recommend as a first effort a two-tiered warning system. Products posing low levels of risks could be listed in a binder available at the store so that individuals who are particularly sensitive to cancer risks can obtain the needed information. Organizations such as Consumers Union also could publish this information. The current 800 number approach might be an analogous alternative. The small group of products posing more serious risks should be given on-product warnings that will indicate to consumers in a visible and readily communicated manner the more significant risks that these products pose. The threshold for dividing these risk groups will depend in part on the distribution of risks in society, which should be explored in a comprehensive manner before implementing the warnings policy. One cannot, for example, grade eggs as being "jumbo" without knowing the size distribution of eggs. Such a policy would convey the differing degrees of riskiness in a more effective manner, while at the same time making available to consumers the information about very low risks should they wish to utilize it in their purchase decisions.

In each case, the wording of the warning cannot be determined in the abstract. Although we know that the California wording is too stringent for an on-product label, the ideal approach would be to test a variety of different warnings with consumers and assess their reactions to them

before embarking on such a major change in our
food risk policies. The cognitive limitations of
individuals in processing information about low
probability events require that we make such an
understanding a fundamental portion of any such
policy development rather than being treated
simply as a minor implementation issue. How we
provide the information and what we tell consumers
lies at the heart of the informational approach
and cannot be viewed as an incidental task.

Perhaps the most important guiding principle is
that our objective is to inform consumers and to
enable them to make better decisions. If we keep
this objective in mind, we will avoid the
distortions created by overly conservative
interpretations of scientific evidence as well as
excessively alarmist warnings that are intended to
jolt consumers into action. The California
initiative has created an opportunity for a truly
major national advance in food risk policy. To
take advantage of this opportunity we must develop
a policy that better reflects an understanding of
how individuals make decisions under uncertainty.

Conclusion

Examination of the principles for hazard
warning policy designs and the alcohol and food
cancer risks case studies indicates that the task
of developing an effective risk communication is
not a trivial undertaking. When engaged in such
an effort, one should be cognizant of the
underlying economic problems that individuals are
attempting to solve. People are making choices
under uncertainty regarding precautionary actions
that they can take to reduce these risks, where
one could include among these precautions a
decision not to use a product at all. Warnings
will play a constructive role to the extent that
they provide new information regarding risks and
precautions in a manner that recognizes the

cognitive limitations that individuals have both
in terms of processing risk information and making
subsequent decisions.

Although it is straightforward to develop sound
guidelines for designing hazard warnings systems,
two major efforts along these lines in the food
and alcohol area have failed to serve as
models for sound warnings efforts. Their major
deficiency is that the structure of the warnings
efforts were not dictated by recognition of the
economic and psychological contexts of the
risk-reducing decisions of consumers. Rather, the
warnings language tended to be dictated by
particular constituency that had lobbied to secure
the initial warnings policy. This intrusion of
political factors on warnings language represents
a major danger that has not yet been generally
recognized in the hazard warnings literature.

It should also be noted that our knowledge of
the manner in which individuals can process
information reliably is still in its nascent
stages. There have been a variety of studies in
recent years documenting inadequacies in risk
perception and shortcomings in individuals'
information processing capabilities. What is
needed is a better understanding of this
intervening cognitive black box to assist in
designing hazard warnings efforts that will remedy
the informational shortcomings that have been
identified.

Notes

1. For an introduction to these issues see Viscusi and Magat (1987).
2. The classic work in this area is by Stigler (1975).
3. See Adler and Pittle (1984).
4. Ibid.
5. Ibid.
6. See Viscusi and Magat (1987).
7. Herbert Simon (1982) coined the "bounded rationality" term.
8. See Viscusi and Magat (1987).
9. See Magat, Viscusi, and Huber (1988).
10. For a broader discussion, see Fischhoff et al. (1981).
11. A more detailed analysis of this issue appears as W. Kip

Viscusi, Testimony before the Subcommittee on the Consumer of the
Committee on Commerce, Science and Transportation, U.S.
Senate, Alcohol Warning Labels, Aug. 10, 1988, pp 84-94, 115-118.
   12. See Hearings before the Subcommittee on the Consumer, op.cit.
   13. Ibid.
   14. Washington Post, Aug. 10, 1988.
   15. 1985 Gallup Poll.
   16. Ibid.
   17. Alcoholism and addiction, July-August 1987, p.10.
   18. 1985 New York Gallup Poll.
   19. U.S. Dept. of Health and Human Services, The Surgeon
General's Report on Nutrition and Health (Washington: U.S.
Government Printing Office 1988).
   20. See Morrall (1986).

References

Adler, R., and D. Pittle, "Cajolery or Command: Are Education Campaigns an Adequate Substitute for Regulation?" Yale Journal of Regulation 2 (1984): 159-194.

Ames, Bruce N., Renae Magaw, and Lois Gold, "Ranking Possible Carcinogenic Hazards," Science 236 (1987): 271-280.

Fischhoff, Baruch, et al., Acceptable Risk, Cambridge: Cambridge University Press, 1981.

Magat, Wesley, W. Kip Viscusi, and Joel Huber, "Consumer Processing of Hazard Warning Information," Journal of Risk and Uncertainty 1 (1988): 201-232.

Morrall, John F., "A Review of the Record," Regulation, 10 (1986): 25-34.

Simon, Herbert, Models of Bounded Rationality Cambridge: MIT Press, 1982.

Stigler, George, The Citizen and the State, Chicago: University of Chicago Press, 1975.

Viscusi, W. Kip, and Wesley Magat, Learning about Risks: Consumer and Worker Responses to Hazard Information, Cambridge: Harvard University Press, 1987.

6

ECONOMIC PRESCRIPTIONS FOR ENVIRONMENTAL PROBLEMS: NOT EXACTLY WHAT THE DOCTOR ORDERED
Robert W. Hahn

Introduction[1]

It is not easy to sit in an ivory tower and think of ways to help solve the world's environmental problems. As one who frequently engages in this exercise, I can attest to this fact. One of the dangers with ivory tower theorizing is that it is easy to lose sight of the actual problems that need to be solved, and the range of potential solutions. In my view, this loss of sight has become increasingly evident in the theoretical structure underlying environmental economics, which often emphasizes elegance at the expense of realism.

In this chapter, I will argue that both normative and positive theorizing could greatly benefit from a careful examination of the results of recent innovative approaches to environmental management. The policies examined here involve two tools that have received widespread support from the economics community--marketable permits and emission charges (Pigou 1932; Dales 1968; Kneese and Schultze 1975). Both of these tools represent ways to induce businesses to search for lower cost methods of achieving environmental standards. They stand in stark contrast to the predominant

"command-and-control" approach in which a
regulator specifies the technology a firm must use
to comply with regulations. Under highly
restrictive conditions, it can be shown that both
of these approaches share the desirable feature
that any gains in environmental quality will be
obtained at the lowest possible cost (Baumol and
Oates 1975).

Until the 1960s, these tools only existed on
blackboards and in academic journals, as products
of the fertile imagination of academics. However,
some countries have recently begun to explore
using these tools as part of a broader strategy
for managing environmental problems. This chapter
chronicles the experience with both marketable
permits and emission charges. It also provides a
selective analysis of a variety of applications in
Europe and the United States and shows how the
actual use of these tools tends to depart from the
role that economists have conceived for them.

The chapter has three objectives. The first is
to provide a comprehensive review of the
experience with these new approaches. The second
is to identify important themes that emerge in the
application of these tools. For example, does the
implementation of emission fees depart from the
economists' prescriptions in systematic ways? The
third objective is to assess how the introduction
of these tools is shaped by broader political
forces that are all-too-often ignored by
economists. By gaining a deeper understanding of
the political environment in which implementation
occurs, we can begin to assess both the potential
and limitations of these new economic approaches.

The Selection of Environmental Instruments

In thinking about the design and implementation
of policies, it is generally assumed that policy
makers can choose from a variety of mechanisms for
achieving specified objectives. These mechanisms

are often referred to as "instruments." While the precise definition of an instrument is somewhat arbitrary, it suffices to think of an instrument as a particular method for achieving a result. Thus, for example, a town may choose between implementing a general sales tax or a property tax as a way of raising needed revenue. In this case, the two taxes may be thought of as different instruments.

Economists have adopted two different approaches to the study of instrument choice. The first, which is normative, examines how to choose the "best" instrument from a given set of instruments. The second, which is positive, attempts to explain how government leaders choose specific instruments in particular situations. Both of these approaches offer important insights that contribute to our understanding of instrument choice.

The hallmark of the normative approach is to specify a desired objective. In the environmental economics literature, this objective is usually stated in terms of minimizing the overall cost of achieving prescribed environmental objectives. The basic insight emerging from the literature is that aggregate pollution control costs will be minimized if businesses and municipalities receive appropriate incentives.

One instrument, which has been shown in theory to supply such incentives, is marketable permits. Implementation of marketable permits involves several steps. First, a target level of environmental quality is established. Next, this level of environmental quality is defined in terms of total allowable emissions. Permits are then allocated to firms, with each permit enabling the owner to emit a specified amount of pollution. Firms are allowed to trade these permits amongst themselves. Assuming firms minimize their total production costs, and the market for these permits is competitive, it can be shown that the overall

cost of achieving the environmental standard will
be minimized (Montgomery 1972).

Marketable permits are generally thought of as
a "quantity" instrument because they ration a
fixed supply of a commodity, in this case,
pollution. The polar opposite of a quantity
instrument is a "pricing" instrument, such as
emissions charges. The idea underlying emissions
charges is to charge polluters a fixed price for
each unit of pollution. In this way, they are
provided with an incentive to economize on the
amount of pollution they produce. If all firms are
charged the same price for pollution, then
marginal costs of abatement are equated across
firms, and this result implies that the resulting
level of pollution is reached in a cost-minimizing
way.

Economists have attempted to estimate the
effectiveness of these approaches. Work by Plott
(1983) and Hahn (1983) reveals that implementation
of these ideas in a laboratory setting leads to
marked increases in efficiency levels over
traditional forms of regulation, such as setting
standards for each individual source of pollution.
The work based on simulations using actual costs
and environmental data reveals a similar story.
For example, in a review of several studies
examining the potential for marketable permits,
Tietenberg (1985, 43-44) found that potential
control costs could be reduced by more than 90
percent in some cases. Naturally, these results
are subject to the usual cautions that a
competitive market actually exist for them to
hold true (see, e.g., Hahn 1984). Perhaps, more
importantly, the results assume that it is
possible to easily monitor and enforce a system of
permits or taxes. The subsequent analysis will
suggest that the capacity to monitor and enforce
can dramatically affect the choice of instruments.

Following the development of a normative theory
of instrument choice, a handful of scholars began

to explore reasons why environmental regulations
are actually selected. This positive
environmental literature tends to emphasize the
potential winners and losers from environmental
policies as a way of explaining the conditions
under which we will observe such policies. For
example, Buchanan and Tullock (1975) argue that
the widespread use of source-specific standards
rather than a fee can be explained by looking at
the potential profitability of the effected
industry under the two regimes. After presenting
the various case studies, I will review some of
the insights from positive theory and see how they
square with the facts.

The formal results in the positive and
normative theory of environmental economics are
elegant. Unfortunately, they are not immediately
applicable, since virtually none of the systems
examined below exhibits the purity of the
instruments which are the subject of theoretical
inquiry. The presentation here highlights those
instruments that show a marked resemblance to
marketable permits or emission fees. Together,
the two approaches to pollution control span a
wide array of environmental problems, including
toxic substances, air pollution, water pollution
and land disposal.

The Slip Twixt the Cup and the Lip

Economic incentive approaches are used to
address a wide variety of environmental problems.
This section provides an overview of some of the
more important applications. The presentation
highlights those instruments that show a marked
resemblance to marketable permits or emission
fees.

Table 6-1 illustrates the wide range of
applications of emission charges and marketable
permits in developed countries. Each column of
the table corresponds to a different application.

Table 6-1

Charges and Marketable Permits: An Overview

Part 1: Charges

Water	Air	Solid Waste	Hazardous Waste	Noise	Products
Australia		Australia			
			Denmark		
		Finland			
France	France	France		France	France
Germany	Germany	Germany	Germany	Germany	Germany
Hungary					
Italy		Italy			
	Japan			Japan	
Netherlands	Netherlands	Netherlands	Netherlands	Netherlands	Netherlands
	Norway	Norway			Norway
		Sweden			Sweden
				Switzerland	
U.K.				U.K.	
U.S.	U.S.		U.S.		U.S.

Part 2: Marketable Permits

Water	Air	Solid Waste	Hazardous Waste	Noise	Products
*	Germany				
U.S.	U.S.		U.S.		

Sources: Barde (1986), Boland (1986), Brown (1984a), Brown (1984b), Brown and Bressers (1986), Hahn (1982), Hahn (1988a), Liroff (1986), Novotny (1986), Sprenger (1986), U.S. Congressional Budget Office (1985)

The table is partitioned into two parts. The
first part shows the countries that are using
various charge systems. Charge systems are
interpreted broadly to include both user charges
and emissions charges. User charges generally
include charges for treating or storing waste,
such as garbage. Emissions charges generally
apply to charges on specific pollutants that are
discharged into the environment.[2] The second part
of the table shows countries which have adopted
some form of marketable permits. The table was
constructed on the basis of available information.
It is not meant to be exhaustive. If a country is
designated as using a particular program, it may
do so on a small or a large scale, depending on
the application. For example, the U.S. makes only
nominal use of air pollution charges in selected
areas. These charges have a relatively small
effect on revenues and no discernible effect on
pollution levels.

The table reveals several interesting points.
First, the use of charges is widespread in the
developed world, in the sense that several
countries have experimented with their use.
Second, the application of marketable permits to
environmental problems appears to be quite
limited. There are only two major applications of
this concept, both found in the United States.
Indeed, there is only one application outside of
the United States that the author has been able to
identify (Sprenger 1986, 18-22). The table also
shows that these approaches have been used to
address a wide range of pollution problems.

Table 6-1 provides an overview of existing
applications, but it does not offer information on
the implementation and performance of various
instruments. To gain a better understanding of
how instruments work, it is necessary to
systematically explore different applications.
The following discussion presents a wide array of
applications in different countries. The purpose

of the analysis is to uncover important trends in
the implementation of these mechanisms. Following
the organization in Table 6-1, selected charge
mechanisms in different countries are examined
first. This is followed by a discussion of the
few existing marketable permit approaches in the
United States.

Charges in Practice
Charge systems in four countries are examined.
Examples are drawn from France, Germany, the
Netherlands, and the United States. Particular
systems were selected because they were thought to
be significant either in their scope, their
effect on revenues, or their impact on the
cost-effectiveness of environmental regulation.
While the focus is on water effluent charges, a
variety of systems are briefly mentioned at the
end of this section which cover other
applications.
   Applications of charge systems are best
understood in terms of the broader regulatory
context in which they are implemented. The cases
reviewed here provide background on the regulatory
structure in which these reforms are initiated.
At the same time, they attempt to summarize
salient features of these instruments that will
yield insights into the political and economic
foundations of environmental policy.

France
The French have had a system of effluent
charges on water pollutants in place since 1969
(Bower et al. 1981).[3] The system is primarily
designed to raise revenues that are then used to
help maintain or improve water quality. Revenues
from the charges are redistributed to the
dischargers through the use of grants, subsidized
loans, and rewards for superior performance (Bower
et al. 1981, 137). In addition, they are used to
help support the basin agencies that administer

the system. Charges cover a wide variety of
pollutants, including suspended solids, biological
oxygen demand (BOD), chemical oxygen demand (COD),
and selected toxic chemicals. Charges, though
widespread, are relatively low. Moreover, charges
are rarely based on actual performance. Rather,
they are based on the expected level of discharge
by various industries. There is no explicit
connection between the charge paid by a given
discharger and the subsidy received (Bower et al.
1981, 126). However, charges are generally
earmarked for use in promoting environmental
quality in areas related to the specific charge.
     Although the majority of charges are based on
average as opposed to individual performance, some
charges are based on actual behavior. If the
activity involves a treatment plant, performance
incentives are related to actual behavior. This
mechanism helps promote more efficient operation
of treatment plants (Bower et al. 1981, 130).
Firms can also ask for individual monitoring of
their behavior if they believe, for example, their
performance is above average. Moreover, if firms
are thought to be exceeding some maximum allowable
value dictated by their permit, penalties can be
imposed. Thus, incentives related to individual
behavior do exist; however, they are rather blunt
in that they do not provide a continuous incentive
to search for lower cost options of abating
pollution.
     There is little quantitative data that can be
used to measure the effect of the effluent
charges; however, there is a general impression
that the system has worked in the sense that water
quality has improved (Bower et al. 1981, 23-24).
While the system may help result in environmental
improvements, the charges do little in and of
themselves to promote cost-effective environmental
improvement. This is because they are relatively
low and are based on average performance rather
than individual performance. Moreover, the

charges are generally based on water intake.
Therefore, the charges do not provide any
incentive for appropriate use or discharge.   The
basic mechanism by which these charges improve
environmental quality is through judicious
earmarking of the revenues for pollution abatement
activities.

In evaluating the charge system, it is
important to understand that it is a major, but by
no means dominant, part of the French system for
managing water quality.   Indeed, in terms of total
revenues, a sewage tax levied on households and
commercial enterprises is larger in magnitude
(Bower et al. 1981, 142).   Moreover, this tax is
assessed on the basis of actual volume of water
used.

Like most other charge systems, the charge
system in France is based on a system of water
quality permits, which places constraints on the
type and quantity of effluent a firm may
discharge.   These permits are required for sources
discharging more than some specified
quantity (Bower et al. 1981, 130).

Charges appear to be accepted as a way of doing
business in France now.   They provide a
significant source of revenues for water quality
control.   One of the keys to their initial success
appears to have been the gradual introduction and
raising of charges.   Charges started at a very low
level and were gradually raised to current levels
(Bower et al. 1981, 22).   Moreover, the pollutants
on which charges are levied has expanded
considerably since the initial inception of the
charge program.[4]

Germany
The German system of effluent charges is very
similar to the French system.   Effluent charges
cover a wide range of pollutants including
settleable solids, BOD, COD, cadmium, and mercury.
The charges are used to cover administrative

expenses for water quality management and to
subsidize projects which improve water quality
(Brown and Johnson 1984, 945).

In 1981, a system of nationwide effluent
charges was introduced (Bower et al. 1981, 226).
Charges have existed in selected areas of Germany,
such as the Genossenschaften, for decades (Bower
et al. 1981, 299). Management of water quality is
delegated to local areas. The federal government
provided the basic framework in its 1976 Federal
Water Act and Effluent Charge Law (Brown and
Johnson 1984, 930). States generally set water
quality standards. Local areas can choose to
implement stricter standards if they desire.

Primary responsibility for implementation and
enforcement of the system is given to the
"Lander", which are the equivalent of states
(Brown and Johnson 1984, 930). Charges are
implemented in conjunction with water quality
permits. The bills that industry and
municipalities pay are generally based on expected
volume and concentration. If a firm meets its
actual standard, it is given a 50% discount.
However, if firms exceed maximum allowable volumes
or concentration, the charge can be raised.
Charges vary by industry type as well as across
municipalities. Charges to municipalities depend
on several variables, including size of the
municipality, desired level of treatment, and the
age of equipment (Brown and Johnson 1984, 938).

Like the French system, it is difficult to
measure the effect of the German effluent charge
system. Initially, charges were opposed by
industry (Brown and Johnson 1984, 932).[5] However,
there is a general perception that the current
system is helping to improve water quality.
Unfortunately, no direct data on the impact of
charges were found. At a minimum, the charge
system serves as an effective subsidy for water
quality management projects.

Netherlands
The Netherlands has had a system of effluent
charges in place since 1969 (Brown and Bressers
1986, 4). It is one of the oldest and best
administered charge systems, and the charges
placed on effluent streams are among the highest.
In 1983, the effluent charge per person was $17 in
the Netherlands; $6 in Germany and about $2 in
France. Because of the comparatively high level
of charges found in the Netherlands, this is a
logical place to examine whether charges are
having a discernible effect on the level of
pollution. Bressers (1983), using a multiple
regression approach, argues that charges have made
a significant difference in the levels of BOD and
heavy metals. This evidence is also buttressed by
surveys of industrial polluters and water board
officials which indicate that charges had a
significant impact on firm behavior (Brown and
Bressers 1986, 12-13). This analysis is one of
the few existing empirical investigations of the
effect of effluent charges on resulting pollution.
Brown and Bressers (1986) note the purpose of
the charge system in the Netherlands is to raise
revenue that is used to finance projects that will
improve water quality. Like its counterparts in
France and Germany, the approach to managing water
quality uses both permits and effluent charges for
meeting ambient standards. Permits tend to be
uniform across similar dischargers. The system is
designed to ensure that water quality will remain
the same or get better. Charges are administered
both on expected and actual levels of discharge.
Actual levels of discharge are monitored for
larger polluters, while small polluters often pay
fixed fees unrelated to actual discharge
(Bressers 1983, 10).
Several pollution measures are used including
COD, heavy metals and nitrogen. One set of
charges is based on a metric defined as
"population equivalent" which represents a

weighted sum of COD and nitrogen. Charges are imposed both on volume and concentration. Revenues from charges on outputs are about fifteen times the revenue from volume charges. There is some variation in charges across jurisdictions. For example, in 1983, there was a threefold difference between the lowest and highest charge (Brown and Bressers 1986, 5).

Charges have exhibited a slow, but steady increase since their inception. This increase is correlated with declining levels of pollutants. Effluent discharge declined from 40 population equivalents in 1969 to 15.3 population equivalents in 1980, and it was projected to decline to 4.4 population equivalents in 1985 (Brown and Bressers 1986, 10). Thus, over 15 years, this measure of pollution declined on the order of 90%.

As in Germany, there was initial opposition from industry to the use of charges. Brown and Bressers (1986, 4) also note opposition from environmentalists, who tend to distrust market-like mechanisms. Nonetheless, charges have enjoyed widespread acceptance in a variety of arenas in the Netherlands. As in Germany and France, charges started at comparatively low levels and then were gradually increased.

One final interesting feature of the charge system in the Netherlands relates to the differential treatment of new and old plants. In general, newer plants face more stringent regulation than older plants (Brown and Bressers 1986, 10). As we shall see, this is also a dominant theme in American regulation.

United States
The United States has a modest system of user charges levied by utilities that process wastewater. Federal environmental regulations issued by the Environmental Protection Agency (EPA) have encouraged the use of these charges. The charges cover a variety of targets including

BOD, COD, and total suspended solids. They are based on both volume and strength, and vary across wastewater utilities. In some cases, charges are based on actual discharges, and in others, a rule of thumb, related to average behavior.[6] In some cases, water quality permits require that pretreatment be performed. Local areas have some latitude in setting the charges provided they conform to federal guidelines. In all cases, charges are added on to the existing regulatory system, which relies heavily on permits and standards.

Both industry and consumers are required to pay the charges. The primary purpose of the charges is to raise revenues to help meet the revenue requirements of the wastewater utilities, which are heavily subsidized by the federal government. The direct environmental and economic impact of these charges is apparently small (Boland 1986, 12). They serve primarily as a mechanism to help defray the costs of the treatment plants. Thus, the charges used in the United States are similar in spirit to the German and French systems already described. However, their size appears to be smaller, and the application of the revenues is more limited.

Other Fee based systems

There are a variety of other fee based systems. Brown (1984a) examined incentive-based systems to control hazardous wastes in Europe and found that a number of countries had adopted systems, some of which had a marked economic effect. The general trend was to use either a tax on waste outputs or a tax on feedstocks that are usually correlated with the level of waste produced. Companies and government officials were interviewed to ascertain the effects of these approaches. In line with economic theory, charges were found to induce firms to increase expenditures on achieving waste reduction through a variety of techniques

including reprocessing of materials, treatment,
and input and output substitution. Firms also
devoted greater attention to separating waste
streams because prices for disposal often varied
by the type of waste stream.

The United States has a diverse range of taxes
imposed on hazardous waste streams. Several
states have land disposal taxes in place. Charges
exhibit a wide degree of variation across states.
For example, in 1984, charges were $.14/tonne in
Wisconsin and $70.40/tonne in Minnesota (U.S. CBO
1985, 82).   Charges for disposal at landfills
also vary widely. The effect of these different
charges is very difficult to estimate because of
the difficulty in obtaining the necessary data on
the quantity and quality of waste streams, as well
as the economic variables.

In addition to taxing waste streams, several
countries impose taxes on products which are
related to waste streams. The United States, for
example, has a system of feedstock taxes on
petroleum and chemical feedstocks. Between 1981
and 1984, these taxes generated over $800 million
in revenues, which will be used to help finance
hazardous waste cleanup under Superfund (Hahn
1988a). While the amount of revenue raised seems
large, the tax is small relative to the price of
the inputs, and appears to have had little or no
effect on firm behavior.

Most of the fee-based systems discussed up to
this point have involved water and hazardous
waste. There are some fee systems related to air
pollution, but they are less prominent. For
example, Sweden has a gasoline tax which increases
with the lead and sulfur concentration of the
gasoline (Brown 1984b). The United States imposes
nominal fees on various emissions to help pay for
some of the administrative costs associated with
regulation. Both Los Angeles and Wisconsin have
nominal fees associated with air emissions (Hahn
1982, 1987a).

The preceding analysis reveals that there are a
wide array of fee-based systems in place designed
to promote environmental quality. The structure of
these systems is remarkably similar in many ways.
Almost all of the fees are used to subsidize some
aspect of environmental quality. In a few cases,
the fees were shown to have a marked effect on
firm behavior; however, in the overwhelming
majority of cases studied, the direct economic
effect of fees appears to have been small. This
is largely due to the fact that fees have been set
at comparatively low levels, and that fees are
often only tangentially linked to the actual
behavior of individual firms.

Marketable Permits
In comparison with fees, marketable permits
have not received widespread use. There appear to
be only four existing environmental applications,
three of which have been implemented in the United
States. One of these applications involves the
control of BOD in a limited river area. The other
three are related to air pollution. One involves
the trading of emissions rights of various
pollutants regulated under the Clean Air Act; a
second involves trading of lead used in gasoline;
a third involves air pollution trading in Germany
and will not be addressed here because of limited
information (see Sprenger 1986). As we shall see,
the performance of these programs exhibits
dramatic differences, which can be traced back to
the rules used to implement the different
mechanisms.

Wisconsin Fox River Water Permits
In 1981, the state of Wisconsin implemented an
innovative program aimed at controlling BOD on a
part of the Fox River (Novotny 1986). The program
was designed to allow for the limited trading of
marketable discharge permits. The primary
objective was to allow firms greater flexibility

in abatement options while still maintaining environmental quality. The program is administered by the state of Wisconsin in accord with the Federal Water Pollution Control Act. Firms are issued five-year permits that define their wasteload allocation along with their initial allocation of permits. Allowable discharges to the river vary over the year as a function of both stream flow and temperature.

Early studies estimated that substantial savings, on the order of $7 million per year, would result after implementing this trading system (O'Neil 1983). However, actual cost savings have been minimal. In the six years that the program has been in existence, there has been only one trade. This trade took place between a paper company and a municipal treatment center (Patterson 1987). Given the initial fanfare about this system, its performance to date has been disappointing.

A closer look at the nature of the market and the rules for trading reveals that the result should not have been totally unexpected. The regulations are aimed at two types of dischargers: pulp and paper plants and municipal waste treatment plants. Approximately 2/3 of the sources are pulp and paper mills with the remaining 1/3 are municipal treatment plants (Patterson 1987). David and Joeres (1983) note that the pulp and paper plants have an oligopolistic structure, and thus may not behave as competitive firms in the permit market. Moreover, it is difficult to know how the municipal utilities will perform under this set of rules, since they are subject to public utility regulation (Hahn and Noll 1983). Trading is also limited by location. There are two points on the river where dissolved oxygen concentrations are critical, and firms are divided into clusters so that trading will not increase BOD at either of these points. There are only about 6 or 7 firms in each cluster (Patterson 1987). Consequently, markets for wasteload allocations may be quite thin.

Novotny (1986) has argued that there are several restrictions on transfers that have a negative impact on potential trading. Any transaction between firms requires modifying or reissuing permits. This takes at least 175 days, and sometimes longer. Transfers must be for at least a year; however the life of the permit is only five years. Moreover, parties must waive any rights to the permit after it expires, and it is unclear how the new allocation will be affected by trading. This creates great uncertainty over the future value of the property right. Added to the problems created by these rules are the restrictions on eligibility for trades. Firms are required to justify the "need" for permits. This effectively limits transfers to new dischargers, plants which are expanding, and treatment plants that cannot meet the requirements, despite their best efforts. Trades that only reduce operating costs are not allowed. With all the uncertainty and high transactions costs, it is not surprising that trading has gotten off to a very slow start.

While the marketable permit system for the Fox River was being hailed as a success by economists, the paper mills did not enthusiastically support the idea (Novotny 1986). Nor have the mills chosen to explore this option once it has been implemented. The approach is best viewed as a very limited form of permit trading. Indeed, by almost any measure, these transferable permits represent a minor part of the regulatory structure. The mechanism builds on a large regulatory infrastructure where permits specifying treatment and operating rules lie at the center. The new marketable permits approach retains many features of the existing standards-based approach. The initial wasteload allocations are based on the status quo, calling for equal percentage

reductions from specified limits. This
"grandfathering" approach has a great deal of
political appeal for existing firms. New firms
must continue to meet more stringent requirements
than old firms, and firms must meet specified
technological standards before trading is allowed.
In this regard, the change is best viewed as
incremental.

Emissions Trading

By far the most significant and far-reaching
program in the United States is the emissions
trading policy.[7] Started over a decade ago, the
policy attempts to provide greater flexibility to
firms charged with controlling air pollutant
emissions. Pollutants covered under the policy
include volatile organic compounds, carbon
monoxide, sulfur dioxide, particulates, and
nitrogen oxides (Hahn and Hester 1986). Because
the program represents a radical departure in the
approach to pollution regulation, it has come
under close scrutiny by a variety of interest
groups. Environmentalists have been particularly
critical of this reform. These criticisms
notwithstanding, the EPA Administrator
characterizes the program as "one of EPA's most
impressive accomplishments," (Thomas 1986).

The Clean Air Act provides the authority for
the regulation of air pollution in the U.S. Two
features of the Act have proved particularly
significant for emissions trading. First, the Act
specifies that every significant source of air
emissions will be regulated individually, and that
different classes of sources will have different
standards applied to them. This has led to large
variations in marginal costs of abatement across
sources. The second significant feature of the
Clean Air Act affecting emissions trading is the
provision that federal agencies determine the
standards and structure of the regulatory system,
but the states implement it. States often did not

have the capabilities or resources to develop
coherent plans for implementing environmental
strategies. Many emissions inventories and
projections were highly inaccurate. This led to a
great deal of controversy over how to define the
nature of property rights which would serve as the
cornerstone of the emissions trading program. The
emission limits contained in operating permits
became the basis for the allocation of property
rights for emissions trading. These property
rights are referred to as "emission reduction
credits."

There are now four distinct elements of
emissions trading. Netting, the first program
element, was introduced in 1974. Netting allows a
firm that creates a new emission source in a plant
to avoid the stringent emission limits that would
normally apply by reducing emissions from another
source in the plant. Thus, net emissions from the
plant do not increase significantly. (However, a
small increase in net emissions may result in some
cases.) A firm using netting is only allowed to
obtain the necessary emission credits from its own
sources. This is called internal trading because
the transaction involves only one firm. Netting
is always subject to approval at the state level,
not the federal.

Offsets, the second element of emissions
trading, are used by new emission sources in
"non-attainment areas."[8] The Clean Air Act
specified that no new emission sources would be
allowed in non-attainment areas after the original
1975 deadlines for meeting air quality standards
passed. Concern that this prohibition would
stifle economic growth in these areas prompted EPA
to institute the offset rule. This rule specified
that new sources would be allowed to locate in
non-attainment areas, but only if they "offset"
their new emissions by reducing emissions from
existing sources by even larger amounts. The
offsets could be obtained through internal

trading, just as with netting. However, they could also be obtained from other firms' sources, which is called external trading. Like netting, offsets are subject only to state approval.

Bubbles, though apparently considered by EPA to be the centerpiece of emissions trading, were not allowed until 1979. The name derives from the placing of an imaginary bubble over a plant, with all emissions exiting at a single point from the bubble. A bubble allows a firm to sum the emission limits from individual sources of a pollutant in a plant, and to adjust the levels of control applied to different sources so long as this aggregate limit is not exceeded. While the trading concept for bubbles is similar to that for netting and offsets, bubbles apply to existing sources. Initially, every bubble had to be approved at the federal level as an amendment to a state's implementation plan. In 1981, EPA approved a "generic rule" for bubbles in New Jersey which allowed the state to give final approval for bubbles. Since then, several other states have followed suit. Banking, the fourth element of emissions trading, was developed in conjunction with the bubble policy. Banking allows firms to save emission reductions above and beyond permit requirements for future use in emissions trading. While EPA action was initially required to allow banking, the development of banking rules and the administration of banking programs has been left to the states.

The performance of emissions trading can be measured in several ways. A summary evaluation that assesses the impact of the program on abatement costs and environmental quality is provided in Table 6-2. For each emissions trading activity, an estimate of cost savings, environmental quality effect, and the number of "trades" is given. In each case, the estimates are for the entire life of the program. As can be seen from the table, the level of activity under

Table 6-2

Summary of Emissions Trading Activity

ACTIVITY	ESTIMATED NUMBER OF INTERNAL TRANSACTIONS	ESTIMATED NUMBER OF EXTERNAL TRANSACTIONS	ESTIMATED COST SAVINGS (MILLIONS)	ENVIRONMENTAL QUALITY IMPACT
NETTING	5,000 TO 12,000	NONE	$25 TO $300 IN PERMITTING COSTS; $500 TO $12,000 IN EMISSION CONTROL COSTS	INSIGNIFICANT IN INDIVIDUAL CASES; PROBABLY INSIGNIFICANT IN AGGREGATE
OFFSETS	1800	200	PROBABLY LARGE	PROBABLY INSIGNIFICANT
BUBBLES:				
FEDERALLY APPROVED	40	2	$300	INSIGNIFICANT
STATE APPROVED	89	0	$135	INSIGNIFICANT
BANKING	<100	<20	SMALL	INSIGNIFICANT

Source: Hahn and Hester (1986)

various programs varies dramatically. More
netting transactions have taken place than any
other type, but all of these have necessarily been
internal. The wide range placed on this estimate,
5,000 to 12,000, reflects the uncertainty about
the precise level of this activity. An estimated
2000 offset transactions have taken place, of
which only 10% have been external. Fewer than 150
bubbles have been approved. Of these, almost twice
as many have been approved by states under generic
rules than have been approved at the federal
level, and only two are known to have involved
external trades. For banking, the figures listed
are for the number of times firms have withdrawn
banked emission credits for sale or use. While no
estimates of the exact numbers of such
transactions can be made, upper bound estimates of
100 for internal trades and 20 for external trades
indicate the fact that there has been relatively
little activity in this area.

Cost savings for both netting and bubbles are
substantial.[9] Netting is estimated to have
resulted in the most cost savings, with a total of
between $525 million and over $12 billion from
both permitting and emissions control cost
savings. The wide range of this estimate reflects
the uncertainty that results from the fact that
little information has been collected on netting.
Offsets result in no direct cost savings in the
sense that the use of offsets does not allow a
firm to avoid any emission limits. However, firms
using offsets probably obtain substantial benefits
from locating new or modified major emission
sources in non-attainment areas, something which
they would not be able to do without the use of
offsets. The fact that firms are willing to go to
the expense of obtaining offsets indicates that
they derive some net gain from doing so, but the
extent of this gain has not been estimated.
Federally approved bubbles have resulted in
savings estimated at $300 million, while state

bubbles have resulted in an estimated $135 million
in cost savings.[10] As these figures indicate,
average savings from federally approved bubbles
are higher than those for state approved bubbles.
Average savings from bubbles are higher than those
from netting, which reflects the fact that bubble
savings may be derived from several emissions
sources in a single transaction, while netting
usually involves cost savings at a single source.
Finally, the cost savings from the use of banking
cannot be estimated, but are necessarily small
given the small number of banking transactions
which have occurred.

The effects that the various program elements
have had on environmental quality are, on the
whole, insignificant. While there have been some
small emissions increases from individual sources
involved in netting transactions, the overall
effect has been inconsequential. For offsets and
bubbles, aggregate effects are also thought to be
insignificant, although they may be slightly
positive. Some transactions may have had an
adverse impact on the environment due to the use
of reductions in allowable (as opposed to actual)
emissions, but their aggregate impact on
individual areas is thought to be inconsequential.
Banking has probably had a slight positive effect,
since banked credits represent emission reductions
which have not been used to offset emission
increases. However, due to the fact that there has
been little banking activity, the total effect of
banking is necessarily very small.

Emissions trading activities have produced a
mixed bag of accomplishments and disappointments.
The program has clearly afforded many firms
flexibility in meeting emission limits, and this
flexibility has resulted in significant aggregate
cost savings--in the billions of dollars.
However, these cost savings have been realized
almost entirely from internal trading. They fall
far short of the potential savings that could be

realized if there were more external trading.   The
scorecard on environmental effects is more
difficult to estimate.   However, the best
available information indicates that the program
has led to little or no net change in the level of
emissions.

The evolution of the emissions trading can best
be understood in terms of a struggle over the
nature and distribution of property rights (Hahn
and Hester 1986, 1987b).   It involves not only
concerns over measurable outputs such as costs and
environmental quality, but also underlying values.
Emissions trading can be seen as a strategy by
regulators to provide industry with increased
flexibility while offering environmentalists
continuing progress toward environmental quality
goals.   Meeting these two objectives requires a
careful balancing act.   To provide industry with
greater flexibility, EPA has attempted to define a
set of property rights that places few
restrictions on their use. However, at the same
time, EPA had to be sensitive to the concerns of
environmentalists regarding the definition of
property rights.   The conflicting interests of
these two groups have led regulators to create a
set of policies that are specifically designed to
deemphasize the explicit nature of the property
right.   The high transactions costs associated
with external trading have induced firms to eschew
this option in favor of internal trading or no
trading at all.

Like the preceding example of the Fox River,
emissions trading is best viewed as an incremental
departure from the existing approach. Property
rights were grandfathered.   Most trading has been
internal, and the structure of the Clean Air Act,
including its requirements that new sources be
controlled more stringently, was largely left in
tact.

Lead Trading

Lead trading stands in stark contrast to the preceding two marketable permit approaches. It, by far, comes the closest to the economist's ideal of a freely functioning market.[11] The purpose of the lead trading program is to allow gasoline refiners greater flexibility during a period when the amount of lead in gasoline was being significantly reduced. The program was designed, in part, to help ease the transition for small refiners. Decreasing the lead content in gasoline meant that most small refiners would need to install new equipment for producing gasoline in order to meet reduced lead content standards while maintaining octane ratings.

Unlike many other programs, the lead trading program was scheduled to have a fixed life from the outset. Inter-refinery trading of lead credits was permitted in 1982. Banking of lead credits was initiated in 1985. The program is scheduled for termination at the end of 1987. Credits are allocated on the basis of the current standard and actual production levels.

The standard has been reduced over time from 1.1 grams/gallon for large refiners in 1982 to 0.1 grams/gallon for all refiners in 1986.[12] Initially, the period for trading was defined in terms of quarters or three-month intervals. No banking of credits was allowed. Rights created in a quarter had to be used or traded in that quarter; otherwise they had no value. Three years after initiating the program, limited banking was allowed, which allowed firms to carry over rights to subsequent quarters. Banking has been used extensively by firms since its initiation. In comparison to other trading programs, the lead program makes little use of the existing permitting structure. This is because the permitting process plays a less direct role in regulating the use of lead in gasoline. Nonetheless, the lead trading program does build

on the existing regulatory structure. The
mechanisms used to monitor the lead content in
gasoline under the old regulatory structure are
also used in helping to monitor lead trading.

The program is notable for its lack of
discrimination among different sources, such as
new and old sources. It is also notable for its
rules regarding the creation of credits. Lead
credits are created on the basis of existing
standards. A firm does not gain any extra credits
for being a large producer of leaded gasoline in
the past. Nor is it penalized for being a small
producer. The creation of lead credits is based
solely on current production levels and average
lead content. To the extent that current
production levels are correlated with past
production levels, the system does acknowledge the
existing distribution of property rights.
However, this linkage is less explicit than those
made in other trading programs.

The success of the program is difficult to
measure directly. It appears to have had very
little impact on environmental quality. This is
because the amount of lead in gasoline is
routinely reported by refiners and is easily
monitored. The effect the program has had on
refinery costs is not readily available. In
proposing the rule for banking of lead rights, EPA
estimated that resulting savings to refiners would
be approximately $228 million (U.S. EPA 1985a).
Because banking activity has been somewhat higher
than anticipated by EPA, it is likely that actual
cost savings will exceed this amount. No specific
estimate of the actual cost savings resulting from
lead trading have been made by EPA.

The level of trading activity has been high,
far surpassing levels observed in other
environmental markets. In 1985, over half of the
refineries participated in trading. Approximately
15% of the total lead rights used were traded.
Approximately 35% of available lead rights were

banked for future use or trading (U.S. EPA 1985b, 1986).

From the standpoint of creating a workable regulatory mechanism that induces cost savings, the lead market has to viewed as a success. Refiners, initially lukewarm about this alternative, have made extensive use of this program. It stands out amidst a stream of incentive-based programs as the "noble" exception in that it conforms most closely to the economists' notion of a smoothly functioning market.

Given the success of this market in promoting cost savings over a period in which lead was being reduced, it is important to understand why the market was successful. The lead market has two important features which distinguish it from other markets in environmental credits. The first, noted above, was that the amount of lead in gasoline could be easily monitored with the existing regulatory apparatus. The second is that the program was implemented after agreement had been reached about basic environmental goals. In particular, there was already widespread agreement that lead was to be phased out of gasoline. What this suggests is that the success in lead trading may not be easily transferred to other applications in which monitoring is a problem, or environmental goals are poorly defined. Nonetheless, the fact that this market worked well provides ammunition for proponents of market based incentives for environmental regulation.

New Directions for Marketable Permits

An interesting potential application for marketable permits has arisen in the area of nonpoint source pollution.[13] The state of Colorado has recently implemented a program which would allow limited trading between point and nonpoint sources for controlling phosphorous loadings in Dillon Reservoir (Elmore et al. 1984).

The state and local water agencies are in charge
of administering the program. The primary purpose
of the program is to improve water quality in the
reservoir. The program was implemented in 1984.
Firms receive an allocation based on their past
production and the holding capacity of the lake.
At this point in time, no trading between point
and nonpoint sources has occurred. However,
trading is expected to take place over the next
five years as treatment plants and developers need
to obtain credits for phosphorous (Overeynder
1987).

As in the case of emissions trading, point
sources are required to make use of the latest
technology before they are allowed to trade. The
conventional permitting system is used as a basis
for trading. Moreover, trades between point and
nonpoint sources are required to take place on a 2
for 1 basis. This means for each gram of
phosphorous emitted from a point source under a
trade, two grams must be reduced from a nonpoint
source (Elmore et al. 1984)).[14] Annual cost
savings are projected to be about $800,000
(Kashmanian et al. 1986); however, projected
savings are not always a good indicator of actual
savings, as was illustrated in the case of the Fox
River.

The EPA continues to experiment with
market-based approaches for a wide variety of
problems. The agency now has pilot programs that
would allow manufacturers of light trucks and
diesel automobiles to trade in particulate
emissions. A similar program for trading between
nitrogen oxides emissions and particulate matter
is being targeted at engines of heavy duty trucks.
EPA has been under pressure to produce a rule that
would allow trading and banking of emission
credits associated with heavy duty engine
emissions. Recently, the Agency put forth a rule
that would allow markets to evolve in rights to
produce chlorofluorocarbons as their use is phased

out (Hahn and McGartland 1988). A similar market approach has been proposed for the phaseout of asbestos (OMB memorandum 1988).

The applications covered in this section illustrate that there are a rich array of mechanisms that come under the heading of emission charges and marketable permits. Table 6-3 provides a summary of these applications. The table is divided into two parts. The first part reviews the experience with specific charges; the second part summarizes various applications of marketable permits. The table illustrates that there is a great deal in common within each instrument class, including the purpose of implementing the instrument, the effect on cost savings, the effect on environmental quality, and the basis for allocating property rights.

One of the striking features of these instruments is that only a handful of the existing options provide incentives for firms to reach an ambient standard in a manner which significantly reduces overall costs. The charge systems are generally designed to raise revenues for specific activities. The marketable permit approaches, while encouraging more efficient forms of pollution control, have for the most part failed to live up to their theoretical potential. The performance of these activities can yield important clues about the potential for judicious development and application of these mechanisms to new problem areas.

Lessons to be Learned

Applications of the textbook definition of charges and marketable permits are all but nonexistent in the real world. It is instructive to explore how actual applications depart from the ideal. This endeavor will help provide the basis for a more informed analysis of policy alternatives. The first part of this section

Table 6-3 Part One

Examples of Charges and Marketable Permits

Part 1: Charges

	France	Germany	Netherlands	United States
Location:	France	Germany	Netherlands	United States
Instrument:	Effluent and User Charges	Effluent Charges	Effluent Charges	User charges levied by wastewater utilities
Medium:	Water	Water	Water	Water
Targets:	TSS, BOD, and COD, soluble salts, toxics, sewage	Settleable solids, COD, BOD, cadmium mercury and toxicity for fish	COD, nitrogen, heavy metals such as cadmium, and suspended solids	BOD; COD; TSS, Volume
Measure:	Expected volume and concentration; sometimes actual	Expected volume and concentration	Actual amounts, except for small firms and households	Volume and strength charges; based on individual and average behavior
Target Groups:	Industry and consumers	Industry, municipalities	Industry and consumers	Industry and consumers
Primary Jurisdiction:	Basin Agency	Lander (states)	Water boards; Ministry of Transport and Public Works	Local areas with plants
Principal Purpose(s):	Raise revenues; subsidize treatment and sewerage projects	Raise revenues	Raise revenues	Help meet revenue requirements
Date of Implementation:	1969	January, 1981 (nation-wide)	1969	EPA regulations encourage from 1972
Activity Level:	Widespread	Widespread	Widespread	Widespread application
Cost Savings:	NA	NA	NA	Apparently small
Environmental Quality:	NA	NA	Marked improvement	Little change

Table 6-3 Part Two

Marketable Permits

Part 2: Marketable Permits

	United States	United States	Fox River, Wisconsin	Dillon Reservoir, Colorado
Location:	United States	United States	Fox River, Wisconsin	Dillon Reservoir, Colorado
Instrument:	Emissions Trading	Lead Trading	Marketable Discharge Permits	Marketable Permits
Medium:	Air	Air	Water	Water
Environmental Targets:	Volatile organic compounds, carbon monoxide, sulfur dioxide, particulates, nitrogen oxides	Lead	BOD	Phosphorous
Measure:	Quantities of emissions, based on actual behavior	Quantity of lead in gasoline	Permits defining allowable discharges during different times of the year	Phosphorous loadings
Target Groups:	Industry	Refiners	Pulp and paper industry, municipal treatment plants	Point and nonpoint sources of phosphorous: industry, developers and treatment plants
Primary Jurisdiction:	Varies by Program - primarily state and local with guidelines set by EPA	Federal	Wisconsin	State and local water agencies subject to federal guidelines
Principal Purpose(s):	Promote flexibility in meeting air quality objectives, reduce costs, speed attainment	Allow firms greater flexibility while meeting more stringent standards	Allow firms greater flexibility while preserving environmental quality	Improve water quality in reservoir
Date of Implementation:	1974 - netting; 1976 - bubbles; 1979 - offsets	Inter-refinery trading, 1982; Banking of lead credits, 1985	1981	1984
Amount of Activity:	Moderate - See Table 2	High	1 trade	None
Cost Savings:	Substantial - See Table 2	Difficult to estimate, but market is very active	Small	None
Environmental Quality:	Little change	No change	No change	No change
Allocation Method:	Grandfathering	Based on current standard and production levels	Grandfathering	Grandfathering
Trading Restrictions:	Technology-based standards, new source requirements, trading ratio	Minimal, must trade within quarter or bank	Must justify need, new source requirements	Technology-based standards, 2:1 trading ratio

NA - not available; BOD - biological oxygen demand; COD - chemical oxygen demand; TSS - total suspended solids

Sources: Boland (1986), Bower et al. (1981), Bressers (1983), Brown (1984a), Brown and Bressers (1986), Brown and Johnson (1984), Elmore et al. (1984), Hahn and Hester (1986), Liroff (1986), Novotny (1986), Patterson (1987), U.S. EPA (1985n).

develops generalizable insights related to the
implementation of charges and marketable permits.
The second part examines how the theory of
instrument choice can benefit by incorporating
some of these insights. The third part assesses
the implications of this analysis for system
design and performance, and offers some
predictions about the future of incentive-based
approaches.

General Patterns in Design and Performance
   One of the key themes in the application of
charges relates to their underlying purpose. The
major motivation for implementing emission fees is
to raise revenues. These revenues are almost
always earmarked for activities that
promote environmental quality. Usually, the
revenues are used to provide subsidies, grants or
loans to private firms and to help support
treatment plants. While the cases presented in
the table are not designed to be representative,
almost all environmental charges that have been
studied in detail appear to be based on a desire
to raise revenues. This is not to say that
incentive effects are not important in some cases.
However, they are not usually the driving force
behind charges. Moreover, up to this point, the
number of charges that have documented effects on
polluter behavior is only a small subset of the
total number of charges.[15] There are several
reasons why existing charges have not had a marked
effect on firm behavior. The first, and probably
most important, is that most charges are not large
enough to have a dramatic impact on the behavior
of polluters. A second reason is that charges are
not always designed to have such an effect. In
particular, many charges are not directly related
to the behavior of individual firms and consumers.
As noted in the table, many are based on expected
behavior, which often is based on the behavior of
the "average" firm in an industry. A third reason

relates to the unavailability of data necessary to
test the hypothesis that charges have led to
environmental improvements.

While charges have not had a major effect on
incentives, they are widely perceived to have had
a positive impact on environmental quality. To
the extent that the revenues from charges are
earmarked for pollution control equipment or
refinements in process technology, this is not
totally unexpected. Indeed, the application of
charge revenues to abatement activities is the
primary mechanism through which charges address
environmental quality. Direct incentive effects
are much less pronounced.

Another feature of charges which is important
in terms of their implementation is that there is
a tendency for the charge to increase over time,
even accounting for inflation. Presumably,
starting out with a relatively low charge is a way
of managing political opponents, and determining
whether the instrument will have the desired
effects.[16]

The application of marketable permits presents
an interesting contrast to that of charges. The
primary motivation behind marketable permits is to
provide increased flexibility in meeting
prescribed environmental objectives. This
flexibility, in turn, allows firms to take
advantage of opportunities to reduce their
expenditures on pollution control without
sacrificing environmental quality. In the case of
emissions trading and lead trading, marketable
permits appear to have given rise to substantial
cost savings. In the case of the Fox River and
Dillon Reservoir, trading has been limited. The
performance of these markets is very much tied to
the rules that govern their operation. In the
case of emissions trading and permit trading on
the Fox River, the level of regulatory involvement
in individual trades is quite high. Moreover,
there are many restrictions on trading. Both of

these features tend to limit the scope for trading, and one of the features observed in both these markets is that their performance has fallen far short of their theoretical potential. In contrast, the lead trading market has enjoyed vigorous levels of activity, and appears to have been very successful, though hard data on the relationship between actual and cost savings are not readily available.

A careful examination of the charge and marketable permits schemes reveals that they are rarely, if ever, introduced in their "pure" form. Virtually all environmental regulatory systems using charges and marketable permits rely on the existing permitting system. This result should not be terribly surprising. Most of these approaches were not implemented from scratch. Rather, they were grafted onto regulatory systems in which permits and standards play a dominant role. While it is true that these alternative approaches are implemented in conjunction with other instruments, it is also important to recognize that the charge and marketable permits systems differ in the extent to which they rely on the existing regulatory apparatus. However, all the systems examined here rely very heavily on the existing regulatory system.

At this point in time, there is a marked difference in the relative utilization of the two types of instruments. Charges currently enjoy more widespread use than marketable permits. Admittedly, it is hard to measure utilization. However, charges are currently used in more individual applications, in more countries, and for more pollutants than marketable permits. It is hard to know whether this trend will continue as experience is gained with both of these instruments.[17]

The level of cost savings resulting from implementing charges and marketable permits is generally far below their theoretical potential.

Cost savings can be defined in terms of the savings that would result in meeting a prescribed environmental objective in a less costly manner. As noted earlier, most of the charges to date have not had a major incentive effect. We can infer from this that polluters have not been induced to search for a lower cost mix of meeting environmental objectives as a result of the implementation of charge schemes. Assuming the current regulatory system departs a great deal from the "ideal" solution yields the result that charges have not performed terrible well on narrow efficiency grounds.[18] The experience on marketable permits is more direct. Hahn and Hester (1986) argue that cost savings for emissions trading fall far short of their theoretical potential. The only apparent exception to this observation is the lead trading program, which has enjoyed very high levels of trading activity.

The example of lead trading leads to another important observation about the efficiency of different charge and marketable permit systems. In general, the two instruments exhibit wide variation in their effect on economic efficiency. Some charges have a marked effect on the generation and disposal of pollutants; others do not. Similarly, some marketable permit approaches have led to significant cost savings while others have not. On the whole, there is more evidence for cost savings with marketable permits than with charges.

The charge systems and marketable permit systems that have been implemented have behaved in a manner which is consistent with economic theory. This observation may appear to contradict what was said earlier about the departure of these systems from the economic ideal. However, it is really an altogether different observation. It suggests that the performance of the markets and charge systems can be understood in terms of basic economic

theory. For example, where barriers to trading
are low, more trading is likely to occur. Where
charges are high and more directly related to
individual actions, they are more likely to affect
the behavior of firms or consumers. At this
point, our knowledge of the behavior of
environmental instruments is largely anecdotal.
One challenge for future research will be to gain
a better understanding of the economic response to
different instruments.

Another important measure of the performance of
these instruments is their effect on environmental
quality. In general, the effect of both charges
and marketable permits on environmental quality
appears to be neutral or positive. The effect of
lead trading has been neutral in the aggregate.
The effect of emissions trading on environmental
quality has probably been neutral or slightly
positive. Charges can affect environmental quality
both directly, through inducing firms to cut back
on pollution, and indirectly, by being used to
subsidize abatement activities. The direct effect
of charges has been modest. Charges are generally
designed to promote environmental quality through
the redistribution of funds to these activities.
The indirect effect of charges on environmental
quality has been significant.

The evidence on charges and marketable permits
points to an intriguing conclusion about the
nature of these instruments. Charges and
marketable permits have played fundamentally
different roles in meeting environmental
objectives. Charges are used primarily to improve
environmental quality by redistributing revenues.
Marketable permits are used primarily to promote
cost savings.

**Towards a More Complete Theory of Instrument
Choice**
The formal theory on the choice of instruments
is noteworthy for its simplicity. It starts from

the premise that bureaucrats and legislators
choose specific instruments to further their own
objectives. The basic insight of these theories
is that the choice of instruments will be affected
in systematic ways by individual perceptions about
the winners and losers from various policies
(Campos 1987; McCubbins and Page 1986).

The positive theory of instrument choice as it
relates to pollution control has been greatly
influenced by the work of Buchanan and Tullock
(1975). They argue that firms will prefer emission
standards to emission taxes because standards
result in higher profits. Emission standards serve
as a barrier to entry to new firms, thus raising
firm profits. Charges, on the other hand, do not
preclude entry by new firms, and also represent an
additional cost to firms. Their argument is based
on the view that industry is able to exert its
preference for a particular instrument because it
is more likely to be well-organized than
consumers.

While this argument is elegant, it misses two
important points. The first is that within
particular classes of instruments, there is a
great deal of variation in the performance of
instruments. The second is that most solutions to
problems involve the application of multiple
instruments. Thus, while the Buchanan and Tullock
theory explains why standards are chosen over an
idealized form of taxes, it does little to help
explain the rich array of instruments that are
observed in the real world.[19] The basic insight
of this work is that the argument that standards
will be preferred to taxes depends on the precise
nature of the instruments being compared. In
particular, under what situations would we be
likely to observe different mixes of instruments?

Another weakness in the existing theory is that
the instruments fail to behave in a way that is
suggested by the theory. The preceding analysis
points to some striking similarities and

differences in the use of these mechanisms. Most emissions charges are used as a revenue raising device for subsidizing abatement activity. Yet, a few also have pronounced direct effects on polluters. Most marketable permit approaches are designed to promote cost savings while maintaining environmental quality. However, existing approaches reveal very different performance characteristics in terms of the degree to which they yield cost savings.

While a complete reconstruction of these theories is beyond the scope of the current paper, it is possible to use information from the case studies to begin to piece together some of the elements of a more coherent theory of instrument choice (Hahn 1988c). One of the key elements in the positive theory is the focus on distributional considerations. This focus is well-placed in that distributional concerns can often provide important clues about the likely range of feasible choices. In the case of charges, it is clear that distributional concerns play an important role in acceptability. While the use of revenue is rarely linked to individual contributions, it is usually earmarked for environmental activities related to those contributions.[20] Thus, for example, charges from a noise surcharge are used to address noise pollution. Charges for water discharges are used to construct treatment plants and subsidize industry in building equipment to abate water pollution. This trend suggests that different industries want to make sure that their contributions are used to address pollution problems for which they are likely to be held accountable. Thus, industry sees it as only fair that, as a whole, they get some benefit from making these contributions. Individual firms in an industry need not receive benefits in direct proportion to their contributions, but overall contributions will generally be earmarked for that industry.

The "recycling" of revenues from charges points
up the importance of the existing distribution of
property rights. This is also true in the case of
marketable permits. The "grandfathering" of
rights to existing firms based on the current
distribution of rights is an important focal point
in many applications of limited markets in rights
(Rolph 1983; Welch 1983). The examples considered
here are consistent with this observation.
Emissions trading and the trading of permits on
the Fox River place great importance on the
existing distribution of rights. Lead trading
places somewhat less importance on the existing
distribution of rights in that it does not
directly grandfather rights to existing
participants. Nonetheless, it does use current
standards as a baseline for determining how rights
are allocated. The bottom line is that all of
these systems place great importance on the status
quo.[21] Charges, when introduced, tend to be
phased in. Marketable permits, when introduced,
usually are optional in the sense that existing
firms can meet standards through trading of
permits or by conventional means. In contrast,
new or expanding firms are not always afforded the
same options. For example new firms which use
state-of-the-art equipment must still purchase
emission credits if they choose to locate in a
nonattainment area. This is an example of a "bias"
against new sources. It results from the fact
that new sources have less of a claim on current
wealth than existing sources. Consequently, they
are asked to pay a higher price in terms of the
environmental costs they will face. While not
efficient from an economic viewpoint, it is
consistent with the political insight that new
sources don't "vote" and existing sources do.
   Though the status quo is important in all
applications studied here, it does not, by itself
explain the rich variety of instruments that are
observed. The fact that instruments perform

differently in terms of both their performance and distribution needs to be explained. To date, very little work has been done in this area.

The status quo defines a distribution of wealth among participants in a political process. It does not speak directly to the underlying preferences of groups and individuals who have a stake in the outcome. By examining these underlying preferences, it may be possible to gain further insights into the nature of instrument choice. Hahn and Hester (1986) have argued that the case of emissions trading can best be understood in terms of a struggle over the underlying property rights. This insight can be extended to the comparison of the lead program and the emissions trading program. The performance of these two programs is directly related to the degree of controversy over the underlying distribution of property rights.

There has been heated controversy over emissions trading since its inception. Several environmental groups have made continued attempts to thwart the expansion of this option. In contrast, there has been comparatively little controversy over the implementation of lead trading. How can we begin to understand the difference in attitudes towards these two programs, both of which had their origins at the federal level in the U.S.?

There are several important differences between these two programs. In the case of lead standards, there appears to be agreement about the distribution of property rights, and the standard that defined them. Refiners had the right to put lead in gasoline at specified levels during specified time periods. Lead in gasoline will be reduced to a final, very low level by the end of 1987. In contrast to lead, there is great disagreement about the underlying distribution of property rights regarding emissions trading. Environmentalists continue to adhere to the

symbolic goal of zero pollution. Industry
believes and acts as if its current claims on the
environment represent a property right.
     In the case of lead trading, output could be
relatively easily monitored using the existing
regulatory apparatus. This was not so for the
case of emissions trading. A new system was set
up for evaluating proposed trades. This was, in
part, due to existing weaknesses in the current
system of monitoring and enforcement. It was also
a result of concerns that environmentalists had
expressed about the validity of such trades.
     The effect that emissions trading was likely to
have on environmental quality was much less
certain than that of the lead trading program.
Some environmentalists viewed emissions trading as
a loophole by which industry could forestall
compliance. Indeed, there is evidence that some
firms may have used bubbles to avoid compliance
deadlines (Hahn and Hester 1986). The effects of
lead trading were much more predictable. Until
1985, there was no banking, so the overall
temporal pattern of lead emissions would remain
unchanged under the program. With the addition of
banking in 1985, this pattern was changed
slightly, but within well-defined limits.
     To accommodate these differing concerns,
different rules were developed for the two cases.
In the case of lead trading, rights are traded on
a one-for-one basis. In contrast, under emissions
trading, rights are not generally traded on a
one-for-one basis. Rather, each trade must show a
net improvement in environmental quality. In the
case of lead, all firms are treated equally from
the standpoint of trading. In the case of
emissions trading, new firms must meet stringent
standards before being allowed to engage in
trading.
     This comparison suggests that it is possible to
gain insights into the likely performance and
choice of instruments by understanding the forces

that led to their creation. Moreover, the general analysis of instruments presented in this chapter has some important implications for existing theories of instrument choice. First, it shows that the view that the choice is dichotomous, (e.g., as between standards and fees), is unnecessarily simplistic. It may very well be the case that the choice can be viewed as continuous for the purpose of theory. For example, in the cases of lead trading and emissions trading, one of the choice variables might be the extent to which market forces should be used for allocating rights. The analysis suggests that efficiency (measured in purely economic terms) may be the by-product of the degree to which groups agree on the underlying distribution of property rights.

This view of efficiency is similar to, but should not be confused with, the notion of efficiency advanced by Becker (1983). Becker argues that government will tend to choose mechanisms that are more efficient over those which are less efficient in redistributing revenues from less powerful to more powerful groups. His argument is based on a model where interest groups compete by exerting influence. Government, in this model, is really a black box that transfers wealth from less influential groups to more influential groups. To the extent that his argument is testable, I believe it is not consistent with the facts. For example, the U.S. currently has a policy that directs toxic waste dumps to be cleaned up in priority order. The policy makes no attempt to examine whether a greater risk reduction could be attained with a different allocation of expenditures. Given a finite budget constraint, this policy does not make sense from a purely economic viewpoint. However, it might make sense if environmentalists hoped that more stringent policies would emerge in the future; or it might make sense if Congress wants to be perceived as doing the job "right" even if only a small part of the job gets done.

A second example that is not easily explained by Becker's theory arises in emissions trading. It is possible to design marketable permit systems that are more efficient and ensure better environmental quality over time (Hahn and Noll 1982; Hahn 1987b). Yet, these systems have not been implemented for a variety of reasons. Environmentalists may be reluctant to embrace market alternatives because they fear it may give a certain legitimacy to the act of polluting. Moreover, they may not believe in the expected results. Thus, for Becker's theory to hold in an absolute sense, it would be necessary to construct fairly complicated utility functions. The problem is that the theory does not explicitly address how important political institutions, such as the legislature and the courts, affect policy making.

Becker (1983, 1985) defends this institution-free analysis in terms of its general applicability and its explanatory power. Yet, the power of the theory is questionable. The essence of the theoretical insight is that efficient redistribution mechanisms will be selected subject to the political constraints that are imposed on the process. At one level, this is simply a tautology. However, as Becker points out, the theory does suggest that more market-oriented (deregulatory) approaches will be selected as the deadweight costs of particular policies increase. I believe this is an important insight, particularly for the type of incentive-based approaches examined here.

Unfortunately, Becker's theory does not offer precise predictions about the impacts of particular policy prescriptions or changes. For example, consider the case of the Gramm-Rudman deficit targets. Becker's theory might suggest that this policy was enacted because the deadweight costs of spending or deficits exceeded some political constraint. However, it is by no

means obvious that Gramm-Rudman will curb the role
of government (which is the prediction one might
expect from his model). Indeed, legislators may
simply substitute other instruments at their
disposal (e.g., regulation, tariffs and quotas) to
achieve their objectives. I argue elsewhere
(Hahn 1988b) that a richer theory, which considers
political institutions, is needed to better
understand the political economy of instrument
choice.[22]

Research that explicitly models the role of
political institutions on the selection of
specific instruments is just beginning to evolve.
For example, Campos (1987) models the instrument
choice problem in terms of maximizing a support
function for a single legislator. While this
approach is elegant, it ignores the role of
bureaucracies in selecting instruments. In the
case of environmental applications, specifically
charges and marketable permits, many of these
ideas originated in the bureaucracy, and some were
implemented without formal authorizing
legislation. Whether these policies were in line
with legislative preferences is not easy to infer.
The point, however, is that it is foolhardy not to
consider bureaucracies as having an important role
in the development and design of many instruments.

In short, existing theories could benefit from
more realism. This realism could be introduced by
a more careful examination of actual applications
of instruments. This means that the mixed nature
of policies would need to be explained. In
addition, the instrument choice problem needs to
be defined more carefully. In the case of the
environment, marketable permits and charges are
only a small part of environmental regulation.
Subsidies and standards represent a major part of
this system, and thus would need to be included in
a more comprehensive theory of policy choice.

The political economy of instrument choice can
benefit from the fact that these choices have now

been been studied in a variety of contexts. As
can be seen from Table 6-1, a large array of
countries use fees; however, only two countries
use marketable permits. Moreover, the application
in Germany is fairly limited. How can this
differential usage of instruments across countries
be explained? Noll (1983) has argued that the
political institutions of different countries can
provide important clues about regulatory strategy.
In addition to institutional structure, which is
undoubtedly important, there are other issues that
may play a key role. The comparison of lead
trading and emissions trading revealed that the
very nature of the environmental problem can have
an important effect on interest group attitudes.

Interest group attitudes can be expected to
vary across countries. In the Netherlands,
Opschoor (1986, 15) notes that environmental
groups tend to prefer charges while employer
groups prefer regulatory instruments. Barde
(1986, 10-11) notes that the political
"acceptability" of charges is high in both France
and the Netherlands. Nonetheless, some French
airlines have refused to pay noise charges because
the funds are not being used (Barde 1986, 12). In
Italy, there has been widespread opposition from
industry and interest groups (Panella 1986, 6-22).
While German industry has accepted the notion of
charges, some industries have criticized the
differential charge rates across jurisdictions.
In the United States, environmentalists have shown
a marked preference for regulatory instruments,
eschewing both charges and marketable permits.
These preferences may help to explain the choice
of instruments in various countries as well as the
relative utilization of different instruments.

The choice set will also be affected by what is
known about the performance of different
instruments. Thus, channels for exchanging
information can play an important role on both the
timing of regulation and the strategy for

regulation. For example, recent applications of
charges in OECD countries may have resulted, in
part, from the success of earlier applications in
other OECD countries. The role of information and
ideas in determining the feasible space of
alternatives is only just beginning to be
appreciated in the area of regulation (e.g., see
Derthick and Quirk 1985; and Brickman, Jasanoff
and Ilgen 1985). It is quite clear that
convincing real world applications or
"experiments" can have important impacts on the
structuring of new policies. For example, in the
case of airlines, there was persuasive evidence
from earlier experience with intrastate
competition that helped pave the way for U.S.
deregulation (Bailey 1986; Levine 1981).

Implications for System Design and Performance
     The review of marketable permits and charge
systems has demonstrated that regulatory systems
involving multiple instruments are the rule rather
than the exception. The fundamental normative
problem is to determine the most appropriate mix.
This mix should be selected in light of the
political realities that have shaped the
implementation of various tools.
     Brown and Johnson (1984) have argued that, in
general, more policy instruments are preferred to
less. This is clearly true in situations where
policy instruments are costless to implement.
However, in the real world, instrument choice
requires tradeoffs among several objectives (Hahn
1986). Moreover, the argument by Brown and
Johnson implicitly assumes that policies will be
used to achieve a given objective. When
objectives of regulatory strategy come into
conflict, the situation is much less clear (Lave
1984). Even when regulatory strategies do not
come into conflict, more instruments may not be
preferred to less.[22] For example, the Netherlands
has decided to combine several charges into one

fuels charge as a means of simplifying the charge system (Opschoor 1986). At this point, all that can be safely concluded is that there is no simple relationship between the number of instruments used and the effectiveness of a policy.

In addition to selecting an appropriate mix of instruments, attention needs to be given to the effects of having different levels of government implement selected policies. The appropriate level of government will be dictated by several factors. One important factor is the scope of the problem. If the problem is local, then the logical choice for addressing the problem is the local regulatory body. However, this is not always true. For example, the problem may require a level of technical expertise that does not reside at the local level, in which case some higher level of government involvement may be required. What is clear from a review of applications of incentive-based instruments is that the level of oversight can affect the implementation of policies. For example, Hahn and Hester (1986) note that a marked increase in bubble activity is associated with a decrease in federal oversight.

The problems of choosing an appropriate level of government for addressing problems and choosing an appropriate menu of instruments for resolving issues are not new. What is new is the information we can now bring to bear on these issue through systematic empirical inquiry into the effects of various instruments and implementation strategies.

The evaluation of existing incentive-based mechanisms has some important implications for their use in the future. Because marketable permit approaches have been shown to have a demonstrable effect on cost savings without sacrificing environmental quality, this instrument can be expected to receive more widespread use. One factor that will stimulate the application of this mechanism is the higher marginal costs of abatement that will be faced as environmental standards are tightened and new environmental issues are added to the regulatory agenda. A second factor that will tend to stimulate the use of both charges and marketable permits is a "demonstration effect." Several countries have already implemented these mechanisms with encouraging results. The experience gained in implementing these tools will stimulate their use in future applications. A third factor that will affect the use of both of these approaches is the technology of monitoring and enforcement. As monitoring cost goes down, the use of mechanisms such as direct charges and marketable permits can be expected to increase.

In the U.S., not only can the use of incentive-based mechanisms be expected to increase, but their form is also likely to change. Increased political pressure to control deficits will induce legislators to design incentive-based systems that yield revenues for the government. In particular, it would not be surprising to see auctions of scarce environmental resources (and other resources, such as spectrum), despite the opposition from well-organized industry groups.[23]

As experience with these approaches grow, they are likely to receive greater support, unless they can be shown to have demonstrable adverse consequences. The "demonstration effect" will be critical in decreasing opposition from industry and environmental groups. Initially, industry has opposed many structural changes in environmental regulation, including both charges and marketable permits. This resistance can be explained, in part, by a type of risk aversion. People and businesses already successfully operating in one environment are often reluctant to make changes which could dramatically affect the "rules of the game" (Allison 1971; Simon 1976).[26]

Conclusions

The preceding analysis reveals that economic approaches to environmental reform are much more complicated than had initially been theorized. However, the performance of both sets of instruments examined here is broadly consistent with economic theory. In the case of permit trading, the performance of the market was integrally related to the rules governing the market. In the case of charges, it appears that incentive effects are important in a few applications. However, in general, charges have tended to serve a revenue-raising function. Marketable permits have served primarily as a mechanism for promoting cost savings.

The study of the politics surrounding environmental reform is in its infancy. This chapter argued that the existing distribution of property rights has a major impact on system design. It also argued that the existing regulatory structure has a major impact on design as well. Most of the systems examined here can be viewed as incremental departures from the status quo, in that they make liberal use of the existing regulatory apparatus.

There is a great deal of work which will be required to construct a more general theory of instrument choice--even a theory which is limited to environmental or social regulation. At this point, it is important to take stock of the progress that has been made to date. Beginning from some stylized definitions of policy instruments that were used for decades in the normative literature on environmental economics, and adopted more recently in the positive literature on instrument choice, we are now at the point where we can provide a better characterization of how different instruments perform in practice. We can also provide partial explanations for the performance of existing instruments as well as partial explanations for their selection. The challenge that lies ahead is to provide a more systematic linkage between the theory and the actual performance of instruments.

Notes

1. This research was funded by the National Science Foundation. The views expressed herein are those of the author and do not necessarily reflect the views of the Council of Economic Advisers.

2. Barde (1986, 13) notes that the distinction between effluent charges and user fees is not always very clear. For example in the case of water, user fees, and effluent charges are closely linked.

3. As used here, effluent charges will be used to denote emissions charges related to discharges into waterways.

4. For example, Brown (1984a, 114) notes that charges for nitrogen and phosphorous were added in 1982.

5. After losing the initial battle, industry focused on how charges would be determined and their effective date of implementation (Brown and Johnson 1984, 932).

6. For example, see Boland (1986, 12). Dischargers using more than 25,000 gallons per day must are required to be charged on their actual use.

7. This analysis of the emissions trading and lead trading programs draws heavily on joint work with Gordon Hester.

8. A non-attainment area is a region that has not met a specified ambient standard.

9. For a detailed discussion of the derivation of these figures, see Hahn and Hester (1986, 43-44 and 50-52).

10. These estimates include savings for bubbles under review as well as those already approved.

11. For a more detailed analysis of the performance of the lead trading program, see Hahn and Hester (1987a).

12. See 47 Fed. Reg. 49322, and 50 Fed. Reg. 9386.

13. Point sources represent sources which are well-defined, such as a factory smoke stack. Non-point sources refer to sources whose emission points are not readily identified. Examples include fertilizer run-off from farms, and water pollution resulting from contamination by animals. Non-point sources are typically more difficult to control than point sources.

14. See Hahn (1987b) for a discussion of the implications of using trading rules that discriminate among different types of sources.

15. Perhaps the best known case is that of the Netherlands (Brown and Bressers 1986). However, there are others. For example Barde (1986, 9) notes that Sweden imposed a tax on fertilizers that caused a drop in consumption.

16. A good analogy to the example of charges is the introduction of the U.S. federal income tax, which started at very nominal levels and then was raised over time. Note, however, that the increases don't necessarily go on forever (thankfully).

17. Within charges themselves, there appear to be some important differences in their application across media, with charges finding greater use for managing water than air. While Table 6-1 does not provide overwhelming support for this view, recall that Table 6-1 does not measure the intensity of the various

applications. The major revenues from charges appear to result from water-related cleanup activities. For example, in the Netherlands, revenues from water-related charges account for approximately 85% of total revenues from charges (Opschoor 1986, 3).

18. Evidence supporting the view that the current U.S. system departs from the ideal is presented in Tietenberg (1985). Although Tietenberg's discussion pertains to the U.S., there is little reason to believe that the systems adopted in other countries are that different in terms of the emphasis placed on identifying economically efficient solutions to environmental problems.

19. Several authors have extended the analysis of Buchanan and Tullock using a similar framework (Coelho 1976; Dewees 1983; Yohe 1976).

20. In his study of the Netherlands, Opschoor (1986, 22) notes that all charge revenues are earmarked.

21. Of course, there may be notable differences among interest groups in defining the status quo. See Hahn and McGartland (1988) for a discussion of this issue in the context of the agreement for reducing chlorofluorocarbons.

22. Though Becker claims to explain a wide variety of deregulatory phenomena, the form of this deregulation is not adequately addressed by his or any other formal theory. The dramatic shifts towards deregulation in industries, such as airlines and trucking, defy a simple explanation. I believe that a complete explanation has to include the payoffs to politicians wishing to appeal to a large segment of the public (specifically, Presidents or politicians aspiring to that office). This payoff is to some extent affected by the state of the economy. It is interesting to note, for example, that Presidential interest in major deregulatory initiatives seems to have increased when the economy was on the skids.

23. Barde (1986, 23) argues that too great a variety of tools amy limit their usefulness.

24. Such approaches would be ideal ways of addressing the "Read-my-lips" pledge of President Bush. They could be justified in terms of "user fees" and the usual arguments about the need for polluters to pay.

25. Indeed, some environmental groups that have long been opposed to incentive-based systems are now taking a second look at both marketable permits and emission fees in specific cases, such as the control of chlorofluorocarbons and acid rain.

26. This resistance to change is not restricted to environmental regulation. See, for example, the discussion of airline deregulation in Derthick and Quirk (1985). An alternative interpretation of this initial resistance is that it represents a bargaining position.

References

Allison, G., The Essence of Decision, Boston, Massachusetts: Little, Brown and Co., 1971.

Bailey, E., "Deregulation: Causes and Consequences," Science 234 (1986): 1211-1216.

Barde, J., "Use of Economic Instruments for Environmental Protection: Discussion Paper," ENV/ECO/86.16, Organization for Economic Cooperation and Development, September 9, 27,

1986.

Baumol, W. and Oates, W., The Theory of
    Environmental Policy, Englewood Cliffs, N.J.:
    Prentice-Hall, 1975.

Becker, G., "A Theory of Competition Among
    Pressure Groups for Political Influence,"
    Quarterly Journal of Economics 98 (1983):
    371-400.

_____, "Public Policies, Pressure Groups, and
    Dead Weight Costs," Journal of Public
    Economics 28 (1985): 329-347.

Bohm, P. and Russell, C., "Comparative Analysis of
    Alternative Policy Instruments," in Handbook of
    Natural Resource and Energy Economics, Volume
    I, edited by A. Kneese and J. Sweeney, New
    York: Elsevier Science Publishers, 395-461,
    1985.

Boland, J., "Economic Instruments for
    Environmental Protection in the United States,"
    ENV/ECO/86.14, Organization for Economic
    Cooperation and Development, September 11, 83
    (1986).

Bower, B. et al., Incentives in Water Quality
    Management: France and the Ruhr Area, Resources
    for the Future, Washington, D.C., 1981.

Bressers, J., "Dutch Environmental Policy," paper
    to be delivered at the International Symposium,
    "Better Environmental Protection for Less
    Money," mimeo, Twente University of Technology,
    Enschede, Netherlands, 1983a.

_____, "The Effectiveness of Dutch Water
    Quality Policy," Twente University of
    Technology, Netherlands, mimeo, 31 pp., 1983b.

Brickman, R., Jasanoff, S. and Ilgen, T.,
    Controlling Chemicals: The Politics of
    Regulation in Europe and the United States,
    Ithaca, New York: Cornell University Press,
    1985.

Brown, G., Jr., "Economic Instruments:
    Alternatives or Supplements to Regulations?,"
    Environment and Economics, Issue Paper,

Environment Directorate OECD, June (1984a):
103-120.

_____, "Selected Economic Policies for Managing
Hazardous Waste in Western Europe," mimeo,
prepared for the Environmental Protection
Agency, August, 36 pp., 1984b.

_____, and Bressers, J., "Evidence Supporting
Effluent Charges," mimeo, September, 28 pp.,
1986.

_____, and Johnson, R., "Pollution Control by
Effluent Charges: It Works in the Federal
Republic of Germany, Why Not in the U.S.,"
Natural Resources Journal 24 (1984): 929-966.

Buchanan, J. and Tullock, G., "Polluters' Profits
and Political Response: Direct Controls Versus
Taxes," American Economic Review 65 (1975):
139-147.

Campos, J., "Toward a Theory of Instrument Choice
in the Regulation of Markets," California
Institute of Technology, Pasadena,
California, mimeo, January 26, 30 pp., 1987.

Coelho, P., "Polluters' Profits and Political
Response: Direct Control Versus Taxes:
Comment," American Economic Review 66 (1976):
976-978.

Dales, J., Pollution, Property and Prices,
University Press, Toronto, Canada, 1968.

David, M. and Joeres, E., "Is a Viable
Implementation of TDPs Transferable?," in E.
Joeres and M. David, eds., Buying a Better
Environment: Cost-Effective Regulation Through
Permit Trading, Madison, Wisconsin: University
of Wisconsin Press, 1983: 233-248.

Derthick, M. and Quirk, P., The Politics of
Deregulation Washington, D.C.: The Brookings
Institution, 1985.

Dewees, D., "Instrument Choice in Environmental
Policy," Economic Inquiry 21 (1983): 53-71.

Dudek, D., and Palmisano, J., "Emissions Trading:
Why is this Throroughbred Hobbled?," Columbia
Journal of Environmental Law 13 (1988):

217-256.

Elmore, T. et al., "Trading Between Point and
Nonpoint Sources: A Cost Effective Method for
Improving Water Quality," paper presented at
the 57th annual Conference/Exposition of the
Water Pollution Control Federation, New
Orleans, Louisiana, 20 pp., 1984.

Hahn, R., Marketable Permits: What's All the Fuss
About?," Journal of Public Policy 2 (1982):
395-411.

_____, "Designing Markets in Transferable
Property Rights: A Practitioner's Guide," in
E. Joeres and M. David, eds., Buying a Better
Environment: Cost Effective Regulation Through
Permit Trading, Madison, Wisconsin: University
of Wisconsin Press, 1983: 83-97.

_____, "Market Power and Transferable Property
Rights," Quarterly Journal of Economics 99
(1984): 753-765.

_____, "Tradeoffs in Designing Markets with
Multiple Objectives," Journal of Environmental
Economics and Management 13 (1986): 1-12.

_____, "Jobs and Environmental Quality: Some
Implications for Instrument Choice," Policy
Sciences, 20 (1987a): 289-306.

_____, "Rules, Equality and Efficiency: An
Evaluation of Two Regulatory Reforms," Working
Paper 87-7, School of Urban and Public Affairs,
Carnegie-Mellon University, Pittsburgh,
Pennsylvania, 1987b.

_____, "An Evaluation of Options for Reducing
Hazardous Waste," Harvard Environmental Law
Review, 12 (1988a): 201-230.

_____, "Instrument Choice, Political Reform and
Economic Welfare," Council of Economic
Advisers, mimeo, November, 1988b.

_____, "The Political Economy of Environmental
Regulation: Towards a Unifying Framework,"
Working Paper 88-33, School of Urban and Public
Affairs, Carnegie-Mellon University, 1988c.

_____ and Hester, G., "Where Did All the

Markets Go?: An Analysis of EPA's Emission
Trading Program," Yale Journal on Regulation
forthcoming, 1987a.
_____ and Hester, G., "Marketable Permits:
Lessons for Theory and Practice," Ecology Law
Quarterly forthcoming, 1988.
_____ and Hester, G., "The Market for Bads:
EPA's Experience with Emissions Trading,"
Regulation 3/4 (1987b):   48-53.
_____ and McGartland, A., "The Political
Economy of Instrument Choice: An Examiniation
of the U.S. Role in Implementing the Montreal
Protocol," Northwestern University Law Review
forthcoming, 1988.
_____ and Noll, R., "Designing a Market for
Tradable Emissions Permits," in W. Magat, ed.,
Reform of Environmental Regulation, Cambridge:
Ballinger 1982:   119-146.
_____ and Noll, R., "Barriers to Implementing
Tradable Air Pollution Permits: Problems of
Regulatory Interaction," Yale Journal on
Regulation 1 (1983):   63-91.
Kashmanian, R. et al., "Beyond Categorical Limits:
The Case for Pollution Reduction Through
Trading," paper presented at the 59th Annual
Water Pollution Control Federation Conference,
October 6-9, 35 pp., 1986.
Kneese, A. and Schultze, C., Pollution, Prices,
and Public Policy, Washington, D.C.:   The
Brookings Institution, 1975.
Lave, L., "Controlling Contradictions Among
Regulations," American Economic Review 74
(1984):   471-475.
Levine, M., "Revisionism Revised? Airline
Deregulation and the Public Interest," Law and
Contemporary Problems 44 (1981):   179-195.
Liroff, R., Reforming Air Pollution Regulation:
The Toil and Trouble of EPA's Bubble, The
Conservation Foundation, Washington, D.C.,
1986.
McCubbins, M. and Page, T., "The Congressional

Foundations of Agency Performance," Public Choice 51 (1986): 173-190.

Montgomery, W.D., "Markets in Licenses and Efficient Pollution Control Programs," Journal of Economic Theory 5 (1972): 395-418.

Noll, R., "The Political Foundations of Regulatory Policy," Zeitschrift fur die gesamte Staatswissenschaft 139 (1983): 377-404.

Novotny, G., "Transferable Discharge Permits for Water Pollution Control In Wisconsin," mimeo, December 1, 19 pp., 1986.

Olivry, D., "Economic Instruments for Environmental Protection in France," ENV/ECO/86.10, Organization for Economic Cooperation and Development, July 9, 84 pp., 1986.

OMB memorandum, "Barriers to Innovation: Alternative Approaches to Regulation," December 12, 12 pp., 1988.

O'Neil, W., "The Regulation of Water Pollution Permit Trading under Conditions of Varying Streamflow and Temperature," in E. Joeres and M. David, eds., Buying a Better Environment: Cost-Effective Regulation Through Permit Trading, Madison, Wisconsin: University of Wisconsin Press, 1983: 219-231.

Opschoor, J., "Economic Instruments for Environmental Protection in the Netherlands," ENV/ECO/86.15, Organization for Economic Cooperation and Development, August 1, 66 pp., 1986.

Overeynder, P., Telephone interview, Consultant to Northwest Colorado Council of Governments, Denver, Colorado, May 26, 1987.

Panella, G., "Economic Instruments for Environmental Protection in Italy," ENV/ECO/86.11, Organization for Economic Cooperation and Development, September 2, 42 pp., 1986.

Patterson, D., Telephone Interview, Bureau of Water Resources Management, Wisconsin

Department of Natural Resources, Madison, Wisconsin, April 2, 1987.

Pigou, A., _The Economics of Welfare_, Fourth Edition, London: Macmillan and Co., 1932.

Plott, C., "Externalities and Corrective Policies in Experimental Markets," _Economic Journal_ 93 (1983): 106-127.

Rolph, E., "Government Allocation of Property Rights: Who Gets What?," _Journal of Policy Analysis and Management_ 3 (1983): 45-61.

Simon, H., _Administrative Behavior_, Third Edition, Glencoe, Illinois: Free Press Press, 1976.

Sprenger, R., "Economic Instruments for Environmental Protection in Germany," Organization for Economic Cooperation and Development, OECD, October 7, 78 pp., 1986.

Thomas, L., Memorandum Attached to Draft Emissions Trading Policy Statement, Environmental Protection Agency, Washington, D.C., May 19, 1986.

Tietenberg, T., _Emissions Trading: An Exercise in Reforming Pollution Policy_, Resources for the Future, Washington, D.C., 1985.

U.S. Congressional Budget Office, _Hazardous Waste Management: Recent Changes and Policy Alternatives_, May, U.S. Government Printing Office, Washington, D.C., 1985.

U.S. Environmental Protection Agency, "Costs and Benefits of Reducing Lead in Gasoline, Final Regulatory Impact Analysis," Office of Policy Analysis, February, 1985a.

U.S. Environmental Protection Agency, "Quarterly Reports on Lead in Gasoline," Field Operations and Support Division, Office of Air and Radiation, July 16, 1985b.

U.S. Environmental Protection Agency, "Quarterly Reports on Lead in Gasoline," Field Operations and Support Division, Office of Air and Radiation, March 21, May 23, July 15, 1986.

Welch, W., "The Political Feasibility of Full Ownership Property Rights: The Cases of

Pollution and Fisheries," _Policy Sciences_ 16
(1983): 165-180.

Wisconsin Department of Development, Division of
Policy Development, Bureau of Research, "Ozone
Air Quality Management and Economic Development
in Southeastern Wisconsin," Report RP-86-8,
October, 1986.

Yohe, G., "Polluters' Profits and Political
Response: Direct Control Versus Taxes:
Comment," _American Economic Review_ 66 (1976):
981-982.

7

DISCLOSURE, CONSENT, AND ENVIRONMENTAL RISK REGULATION
F. Reed Johnson

Introduction[1]

The regulatory apparatus for controlling
environmental risks is designed primarily to
identify safe exposure thresholds and enforce
controls based on that standard.
Unfortunately this system is ill-suited to deal
with several categories of risk. One category
includes hazards for which the public's concern
seems disproportionately large relative to the
actual risks. These include toxic waste dumps,
potentially contagious medical wastes, pesticide
residuals in food, and possibly nuclear power.
Another category includes hazards for which the
public's concern seems disproportionately small
relative to the actual risks involved. Naturally
occurring carcinogens in food, and natural hazards
from floods, earthquakes, and hurricanes are
examples. A third category consists of hazards
beyond the reach of conventional regulatory
enforcement, such as indoor air quality in private
residences.
It is natural to think of information as a

positive good. Information should   lead to
better decisions, increasing the welfare
attainable with limited resources. However,
this simplistic view does not provide a
particularly useful framework for understanding
the role of disclosure in a regulatory context.
The usual rationale for public information
programs is that they will motivate people to
reduce risks voluntarily. However, public
officials sometimes resist such efforts because of
the concern that disclosure will create
unnecessary and inappropriate anxiety on the part
of the public. Other regulators argue that
disclosure appears to have no affect on public
apathy (Adler and Pittle 1978). In both
situations a more-or-less informed public appears
inclined to reject established health standards.
This result is troublesome to environmental policy
makers who are concerned with improving aggregate
public health.

This chapter discusses some practical and
ethical dilemmas facing government agencies
charged with protecting the public health and
safety from such hazards. The analysis focuses on
the role of government as an information
provider in light of discrepancies between public
health objectives and public attitudes about
health risks. The chapter explores the economic
welfare implications of different regulatory
perspectives by modeling preferences under
alternative disclosure frames.

Informed Consent and Risk Regulation

The conventional public health or
standard-setting approach to health risk
regulation occupies a gray area between the
technical and the political. Standards convey
the implicit message that risks are insignificant
below and unacceptable above a specified norm and
therefore require regulators to apply some

standard of social acceptability. However, citizens' willingness to accept expert judgement on appropriate standards appears to vary with characteristics of the risk other than simple probabilities. Public health regulators frequently find themselves trying to justify their decisions to a public that is sometimes apathetic and sometimes angry and skeptical.

The narrow technical definition of health risk in technical risk assessments partly explains the apparent discrepancy in public perceptions. Risk assessments typically treat all deaths of equal value. However, the public appears not to regard death from emphysema the same as death from lung cancer, or the death of an elderly person the same as a death from fatal birth defects. Slovic et al.'s (1985) well-known taxonomy of risk characteristics suggests that health risks enter into individual utility functions differently than public health regulators implicitly assume.

An alternative regulatory approach explicitly distinguishes between a passive public that is subject to risks and an active public that takes risks. This approach acknowledges the absence of a meaningful zero-risk threshold and the fact that risk preferences vary substantially among people. Analogous to the caveat-emptor approach to consumer purchases, people are obligated to assess their own risks and determine the protective response most consistent with their preference for safety relative to other goods. Government's role is limited to disseminating information in a form most useful in making personal risk choices. The normative appeal of caveat emptor rests on the assumption of the perfectly informed, rational consumer. The sometimes apathetic, sometimes angry public that public health officials face also poses problems for the caveat emptor approach when the response appears inconsistent with this assumption.

Both regulatory approaches rely implicitly on information disclosure as a means of achieving regulatory goals.   Although economists have addressed the value of information in the context of intertemporal decisions (see for example Viscusi 1984; Bishop 1982; Graham 1981; and Schmalensee 1972), economists have neglected benefit-cost analysis of criteria for the dissemination of information.

Public risk perceptions pose problems for regulators when experts regard the reaction of ordinary citizens as misguided or inappropriate in view of the actual nature and magnitude of the risk (Slovic et al. 1985; Svenson and Fischhoff 1985).   The public health or standard-setting approach attempts to circumvent individual perceptions by imposing expert judgment about what policies are appropriate to protect public health. The economic or caveat-emptor approach takes individual, subjective utility as primary. Welfare is inherently subjective.   If people feel worse off, the economist accepts that they are worse off.[2]   However, perceived welfare based on incomplete or counterfactual information undermines the normative value of caveat emptor.

The communication interface between government regulators and the public is in many ways analogous to that between physician and patient.   The physician is responsible for guiding the technically uninformed patient in choosing among alternative medical treatments.   The physician, in turn, has limited information about patient preferences and perceptions.   The well-known economic literature on principal-agent models has explored problems of incentives and monitoring in relationships characterized by such asymmetric information (see for example Harris and Raviv 1978; and Holmstrom 1984).   A related literature has evolved regarding informed consent in medicine and human-subjects research (Faden and Beauchamp 1986).   This literature

attempts to define appropriate constraints on an
agent's decisions and actions that directly
affect a patient's or subject's welfare. The
ethical basis for informed consent is the
principle of respect for individual autonomy.
    The standard-setting approach to regulatory
policy is not based on the principle of respect
for autonomy, but on the principle of
beneficence--specifically minimizing the
incidence of morbidity and mortality in the
population. In contrast, economists usually agree
that ideal government regulation of health risks
should shield people from hazards to the degree
they would have chosen for themselves if they
were fully informed and had the means of avoiding
exposure. Therefore the caveat emptor approach
appears to be more consistent with the standard of
informed consent.
    Faden and Beauchamp (1986) establish four
prerequisites for informed consent:

    1)   The agent completely discloses the nature
          of the action and the foreseeable
          consequences and likely outcomes that
          might follow.
    2)   The subject comprehends the disclosure.
    3)   The subject acts voluntarily in
          authorizing the intervention.
    4)   The subject is competent to authorize the
          intervention.

The practical significance of these prerequisites
has been widely debated. Most formal consent
requirements emphasize only the first condition.[3]
A national commission report argued that subjects
are generally incapable of weighing risk-benefit
ratios, so that "full protection of subjects'
rights is assured only when the Institutional
Review Board, not the subject, determines whether
the subject is at risk" (Veatch 1979). Although
complete disclosure may be hard enough to

achieve, provision of information alone does not
ensure informed consent.

In a regulatory context MacLean (1986) suggests
that there is a spectrum of consent associated
with risks. At one end of the spectrum, consent
is actual and explicit. At the other end of the
spectrum, consent is implicit or hypothetical.
Maclean raises ethical questions about the
legitimacy of public policies that rely on
hypothetical consent, even though it may be
impossible to disclose all relevant information
to all affected people, much less satisfy the
other conditions for fully informed consent.

However, one should distinguish uninformed
beliefs from contestable beliefs. Suppose
homeowners discover an illegal hazardous waste
disposal site in their neighborhood. They
begin to attribute the occurrence of certain
illnesses to exposure to the wastes. Experts
agree that these conditions cannot medically be
attributed to their exposure. After
receiving careful explanation of the relevant
toxicology, the people may understand that the
experts think that their health has not been
adversely affected, but may nevertheless
continue to believe that it has. This belief
might well lead to aversive behavior and
measurable economic losses. It is possible that
circumstances satisfy all four prerequisites for
informed consent (in this case denial). Respect
for autonomy requires accepting the homeowners'
perceived welfare as a legitimate basis for public
policy. However, regulatory authorities are
likely to disregard their perceptions if policy
is based on protecting public health.

In most cases the information available to
both regulators and the public at any moment is
imperfect and incomplete. Although the quantity
and quality of available information changes over
time, citizens must act on their perception of
the completeness and accuracy of information

available to them at any given moment. It follows
that they will regard some private
environmental-risk decisions as mistaken in
retrospect.[4] However, it is not a foregone
conclusion that perceptions will converge with
expert opinion over time.

Even when communication with affected people
is feasible, accurate and complete disclosure has
proven very difficult to achieve. Investigators
in both clinical and field experiments have shown
that framing, format, and tone of disclosure
messages affect how people understand and use
risk information. There is abundant evidence
from many clinical and a few field experiments
that perceptions are influenced by how risks and
related choices are described. Tversky and
Kahneman (1981) concluded an influential article
on the psychology of risk perceptions with the
following observation:

> The framing of an action sometimes affects the
> actual experience of its outcomes. For
> example, framing outcomes [in particular
> ways] ... may attenuate one's emotional
> response to an occasional loss. ... The
> framing of acts and outcomes can also reflect
> the acceptance or rejection of responsibility
> for particular consequences. ... When framing
> influences the experience of consequences, the
> adoption of a decision frame is an ethically
> significant act. [p. 458]

Tversky and Kahneman have shown that even expert
opinion is vulnerable to such framing effects.

Weinstein, Sandman, and Roberts (1988)
recently compared information materials on radon
and asbestos. They tested various visual formats
depicting the risk of exposure to these hazards.
Elicitations of illness probabilities,
acceptable risk levels, threat perceptions, and
mitigation plans were similar in separate trials

when the EPA standard appeared about in the
middle of a risk chart, even though the radon
standard is twenty-five times riskier than the
asbestos standard.[5] They also detected a mild
discontinuity around the standard, i.e., the
tendency to indicate concern for the problem
increased more rapidly as risks increased
from just below the standard to just above the
standard.

In an ongoing field experiment Smith et al.
(1987, 1988) have shown that standard-setting and
caveat-emptor formats induce differences in
learning, formation of risk perceptions, and
intended or recommended behavior. Consistent with
the Weinstein et al. findings, the field
experiment has yielded evidence of a perceptual
discontinuity around the standard. Subjects
received actual results of radon monitoring in
their living area and basement together with one
of several variants of an information brochure.
Subjects who had received a version of a brochure
that emphasized the categorical nature of the
federal standard without quantitative information
on the associated risks appeared to treat the
standard as a threshold. When the basement
reading crossed the threshold, perceptions of the
risk increased measurably.

If attempts to inform people lead to different
behavioral responses under objectively identical
circumstances, then public agencies should
evaluate the social and political implications of
such programs at least as carefully as they
evaluate the regulations themselves. We
can expect that an information disclosure program
based on the standard-setting assumptions will
yield different perceptions and behavior than one
based on caveat-emptor assumptions.

A Model of Welfare Under Alternative Disclosure Frames

Several recent studies have attempted to extend the standard model of consumer behavior to incorporate imperfect and changing information on health risks. Shulstad and Stoevener (1978) analyzed the effect of newspaper accounts of mercury contamination of Oregon pheasants on hunting activity. Schwartz and Strand (1981) investigated the effect of publicity about kepone contamination of James River oysters on shellfish demand. Ippolito and Ippolito (1981, 1983, 1985) addressed the role of increased awareness of smoking risks in reducing smoking in the context of a dynamic model of consumption behavior. Foster and Just (1988) extended the basic results on consumer welfare measures to incorporate changing quantity and quality of information over time. They used the model to estimate consumer losses that resulted from publicity on heptachlor contamination of milk in Hawaii. The following discussion elaborates and extends their approach to explore the implications for risk regulation.

Let Z represent information that may influence the subjective probability distribution parameters of the risk q associated with a private consumption good x. An example could be information about the connection between certain consumption patterns and adverse health consequences. Let q be a random variable distributed with subjective mean $m=g(Z)$ and subjective variance $s=h(Z)$. Utility is a well-behaved function $U[x(q),y]$, where y is a composite good.

The consumer maximizes expected utility subject to an income constraint:

$$V(P,Z,m) = \max_{x,y} \{E_z[U(x(q),y)] : p_x x + p_y y \leq M\}$$

where $V(\cdot)$ is the indirect expected utility
function, E_z is the expectation operator relative
to the subjective distribution parameters of q,
p_x and p_y are prices, and M is income.[6]
Foster and Just (1988) derive the intuitively
reasonable results that $\partial x/\partial m < 0$ and $\partial x/\partial s < 0$
under standard assumptions.

Let (x_c, y_c) be the chosen consumption bundle
when the regulatory authority frames its message
in a caveat emptor or full disclosure context,
Z_c. Suppose the standard-setting frame, Z_s,
yields a chosen consumption bundle (x_s, y_s) that
maximizes health. If there is no further
disclosure and characteristics of x other than
health risk enter utility, then the problem is
analytically similar to quantity rationing.
Framing the available information as a health
standard prohibits the adjustment from x_s to
x_c. However, in this case the rationed commodity
is risk information, a public good that happens to
be a complement to private good x.

Figure 7-1 illustrates the effect of framing
when the consumer is more averse to the risk than
public health concerns alone would dictate. U_s^o
is the initial utility index under the standard
presuming only health affects utility, where the
superscript indicates the utility level and the
subscript indicates the information frame. The
corresponding utility under the full disclosure
frame is U_c^o, which has the same utility index as
U_s^o but incorporates risk perceptions.
Disclosure and full adjustment would lead to
utility U_c^* at consumption x_c. From the
public-health perspective the consumer is worse
off at the lower utility level U_c^*. From the
informed-consent perspective the consumer is
better off at the higher utility level U_c^*
(relative to the information-constrained level
U_c').

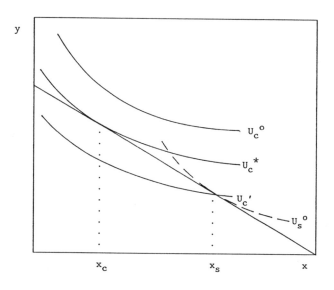

Figure 7-1

In the context of ordinary quantity rationing, Neary and Roberts (1984) use a standard supporting hyperplane theorem to prove that there exists some "virtual" price p_{xs} that supports (x_s, y_s). Extending their argument to the present case,

$$V(P, Z_s, M) \geq V(P, Z_c, M) \text{ implies}$$

$$p_{xs}x_c + p_y y_c \geq p_{xs}x_s + p_y y_s.$$

In other words, the virtual price induces the consumer to demand the same x under complete disclosure as he consumes under the health standard at price px.

Introducing the expectation operator into the otherwise familiar expenditure function yields:

$$e(P, Z, U) = \min_{x,y} \{p_x x + p_y y : E_z[U(x(q), y)] \geq U\}.$$

The partial derivatives of $e(\cdot)$ with respect to p_x and p_y are the compensated demands x_u and y_u for given Z in the stochastic as well as the nonstochastic case (see Just, Hueth, and Schmitz 1982).

To investigate the effect on expenditure of a change in disclosure frame, denote the constrained expenditure function as $e'(P,Z,U,x_s)$. The partial derivative of $e'(\cdot)$ with respect to p_y is the constrained compensated demand y_u'. It follows that

$$e(P,Z_s,U_s^{\,o}) = e'(P,Z_c,U_c^{\,o},x_s) = p_x x_s$$

$$+ \; p_y y_u'(P,Z_c,U_c^{\,o},x_s)$$

$$= p_x x_u(P_s,Z_c,U_c^{\,o}) \; + \; p_y y_u(P_s,Z_c,U_c^{\,o})$$

$$= p_x x_u(P_s,Z_c,U_c^{\,o}) \; - \; p_x x_u(P_s,Z_c,U_c^{\,o})$$

$$+ \; p_x x_u(P_s,Z_c,U_c^{\,o}) \; + \; p_y y_u(P_s,Z_c,U_c^{\,o})$$

$$= e(P_s,Z_c,U_c^{\,o})$$

$$+ (p_x - p_{xs})\, x_u(P_s,Z_c,U_c^{\,o}) \, .$$

Thus the difference between expenditure under the public-health frame and the compensated expenditure at the virtual price under full disclosure is simply the difference in actual and virtual price times public-health quantity.

Reductions in required expenditures for given utility increase welfare for given income. Figure 7-1 corresponds to the case where the full-disclosure frame increases the mean of perceived risk relative to the health standard. Higher perceived risk causes $x_c < x_s$ and therefore $p_x > p_{xs}$. The expenditure necessary to achieve a given level of utility increases and consumers are worse off relative to public-health utility. If change in frame decreases the perceived mean (or

decreases the variance), then required expenditure
decreases.

A common framing problem occurs when
information is provided in the context of
disagreement among experts or if the information
format is confusing or contradictory. Such
a situation is especially likely if the news media
are an important information channel. Regardless
of whether perceived mean risk increases or
decreases, behavior may be dominated by the
tendency to decrease risky activities in
response to increased uncertainty about the
reliability of the risk information. As we
indicated previously, such a situation poses
problems for informed consent advocates. It
is unclear what form "full disclosure" should take
under these conditions. In any case, resulting
movements away from the public health standard
result in the same pattern of welfare effects as a
change in the mean risk alone.

Conclusions

Risk perception is a complex cognitive
phenomenon. People apparently employ a variety of
filters to transform and interpret information in
light of certain preconceptions, attitudes, and
information-processing abilities. This process
does not necessarily mean that people behave
irrationally. It is clear in other areas that
people do not maximize their health to the
exclusion of other considerations. People who
smoke, do not buckle seat belts, eat fatty,
high-cholesterol foods, ride motorcycles, etc.
justify their actions by the enjoyment they gain
from such activities. If they are fully informed
about the potential health consequences, then
their decisions presumably reflect a subjective
assessment that the benefits of risky behavior
exceed the costs.

If the goal of public policy is to maximize

individual and social welfare, then we should permit people to trade their personal health for more desired goods. This view implies that the appropriate measure of an information program's success is not whether everyone above some (arbitrary) exposure level takes action to reduce their exposure, but whether people fully understand the consequences of taking or not taking action. The consequences of living in a house with given radon levels might be very different for a family with young children compared to a single elderly person.

Public health regulators typically regard disclosure as a relatively simple public relations effort to explain an agency's regulatory decisions. We have suggested that there are both practical and ethical problems with this approach. Informed consent provides an ethically attractive alternative model for public information programs. The difference in these two regulatory approaches implies different implicit specifications of individual utility. Economists are generally more willing to allow people to trade off health for other values and are more willing to disclose information to facilitate such tradeoffs. The disagreement on how to measure welfare explains much of the bureaucratic tension between traditional public health officials and managers and analysts who ascribe to the principle of informed consent.

NOTES

1. The views expressed are those of the author and should not be attributed to the Department of Defense or the U.S. Environmental Protection Agency.

2. The Supreme Court rejected this principle in litigation relating to the Three Mile Island accident. In his concurring decision Justice Brennan wrote:

"There can be no doubt that psychological injuries are cognizable under NEPA..., however the particular psychological injury alleged in this case did not arise, for example, out of direct sensory impact of a change in the physical environment..., but out of a perception of risk... . (Quoted in Hartsough and Savitsky 1984).

3. Under Food and Drug Administration rules, "'Consent' or 'informed consent'

means that the person involved has legal capacity to give consent, is so situated
as to be able to exercise free power of choice, and is provided with a fair
explanation of all material information concerning the administration of the
investigation drug, or his possible use as a control, as to enable him to make an
understanding decision as to his willingness to receive said investigational drug.
This latter element requires that before the acceptance of an affirmative decision
by such person the investigator should make known to him ... [a long list of items
to be disclosed follows]." Federal Register, 31, 1966. 11415.
     4. The effects on rational choice of this possibility have been formalized in
so-called regret theory by Loomes and Sugden (1982).
     5. The EPA radon guideline is a technology-based rather than a health-based
standard. However, the media has treated it generally as a safety standard.
     6. Recent challenges to expected utility models (see Schoemaker 1982) need
not invalidate this approach. Freeman (1989) has recently shown that non-expected
utility specifications pose no special difficulties for deriving welfare measures
of risk. The model presented here introduces   consumer reaction to health risk
information in a very general way. Consumers are only required to prefer less of
the good as perceived risks increase.

REFERENCES

Adler, Robert S. and R. David Pittle. "Cajolery or
     Command: Are Education Campaigns an Adequate
     Substitute for Regulation?" Yale Journal on
     Regulation 1 (1984): 159-193.
Bishop, R.C. "Option Value: An Exposition and
     Extension." Land Economics 58 (February 1982):
     1-15.
Faden, Ruth R. and Tom L. Beauchamp. A History
     and Theory of Informed Consent. New York:
     Oxford University Press, 1986.
Foster, W. and R.E. Just. "Consumer Valuation of
     Health Risk: The Case of Heptachlor
     Contamination of Milk in Hawaii." Journal of
     Environmental   Economics and Management, in
     press, 1989.
Freeman, A. Myrick III. "Valuing Individual's
     Changes in Risk: A General Treatment."
     Discussion Paper QE89-08, Resources for the
     Future, 1989.
Graham, D.A. "Cost-Benefit Analysis under
     Uncertainty." American Economic Review 71
     (September 1981): 715- 725.
Harris, Milton and Raviv, Artur. "Some Results on
     Incentive Contracts with Applications to

Education and Employment, Health Insurance, and Law Enforcement." <u>American Economic Review</u> 68 (March 1978) 20-30.

Hartsough, Don M. and Jeffrey C. Savitsky. "TMI: Psychology and Environmental Policy at a Crossroads." <u>American Psychologist</u> 39 (October 1984): 1113-22.

Holmstrom, Bengt. "On the Theory of Delegation," in M. Boyer and R. Kihlstrom, eds. <u>Bayesian Models in Economic Theory</u>. Amsterdam: Elsevier North-Holland, 1984.

Ippolito, Pauline M. "Information and the Life Cycle Consumption of Hazardous Goods." <u>Economic Inquiry</u> 19 (October 1981):529-558.

_____ and Ippolito, Richard A. "Measuring the Value of Life from Consumer Reactions to New Information." <u>Journal of Public Economics</u> 25 (1983): 53-81.

_____. "Valuing Life Savings." Proceedings of the Society for Risk Analysis Annual Meeting, 1985.

Just, Richard E., Darrell L. Hueth, and Andrew Schmitz. <u>Applied Welfare Economics and Public Policy</u>. Englewood Cliffs: Prentice-Hall, Inc., 1982.

Loomes, Graham and Robert Sugden. "Regret Theory: An Alternative Theory of Rational Choice under Uncertainty." <u>Economic Journal</u> 92 (December 1982): 805-24.

MacLean, Douglas. "Risk and Consent: Philosophical Issues for Centralized Decisions," in Douglas MacLean, ed. <u>Values at Risk</u>. Totowa, N.J.: Rowman and Allanheld. 1986.

Neary, J.P. and Roberts, K.W.S. "The Theory of Household Behaviour Under Rationing." <u>European Economic Review</u> 13 (January 1980): 25-42.

Schmalensee, R. "Option Demand and Consumer's Surplus: Valuing Price Changes under Uncertainty." <u>American Economic Review</u> 62 (December 1972): 813-824.

Schoemaker, P.J. "The Expected Utility Model: Its
    Variants, Purposes, Evidence and Limitations."
    Journal of Economic Literature 20 (June 1982):
    529-563.
Schulstad, R.N. and H.H. Stoevener. "The Effects
    of Mercury Contamination in Pheasants on the
    Value of Pheasant Hunting in Oregon." Land
    Economics 54 (February 1978): 39-49.
Schwartz, D.G. and I.E. Strand. "Avoidance Costs
    Associated with Imperfect Information: The
    Case of Kepone." Land Economics 57 (May 1981):
    139-150.
Slovic, Paul, Baruch Fischhoff, and Sarah
    Lichtenstein. "Regulation of Risk: A
    Psychological Perspective," in Regulatory
    Policy and the Social Sciences, Roger Noll,
    ed. Berkeley, California: University of
    California Press, 1985.
Smith, V. Kerry, William H. Desvousges, Ann
    Fisher, and F. Reed Johnson. "Communicating
    Radon Risk Effectively--A Mid-Course
    Evaluation." U.S. Environmental Protection
    Agency Report   EPA-230-07-87-029, Washington,
    D.C.: June 1987.
_____, William H. Desvousges, F. Reed Johnson,
    Ann Fisher. "Can Public Information Programs
    Affect Risk Perceptions?" unpublished
    manuscript, 1988.
Svenson, Ola and Baruch Fischhoff. "Levels of
    Environmental Decisions," Journal of
    Environmental Psychology 5 (1985): 55-67.
Tversky, Amos and Daniel Kahneman. "The Framing of
    Decisions and the Psychology of Choice."
    Science 211 (1981); 453-458.
Viscusi, W. Kip. "Regulating Uncertain Health
    Hazards When There is Changing Information."
    Journal of Health Economics 3 (December 1984):
    259-273.
Veatch, R. "The National Commission
    Recommendations on Institutional Review
    Boards." Hastings Center Report 9 (1979)

22-23.
Weinstein, Neil D., Peter M. Sandman, and Nancy E.
    Roberts. "Communicating Effectively about
    Changes in Risk." Report to the U.S.
    Environmental Protection Agency, Office of
    Policy Analysis, November 1988.

INDEX

Adler, R., 8, 128n, 190
Allison, G., 179
Bailey, E., 59, 176
Barde, J., 176, 180n, 182n
Baseman, K., 80n
Baumol, W., 55, 59, 79n, 132
Beauchamp, T., 192, 193
Becker, G., 2, 17, 26n, 31, 51n, 61, 80n, 173, 174, 181n
Berg, S., 79n
Bishop, R., 192
Boland, J., 144, 180n
Bower, B., 138-141
Braeutigam, R., 80n
Brennan, G., 20
Bressers, J., 142, 143, 181n
Brickman, R., 176
Brown, G., 141-145, 177, 180n
Buchanan, J., 2, 10n, 20, 31, 51n, 135, 167
Cabe, R., 80n
Campos, J., 167, 174
Carron, A., 21
Crandall, R., 51n
Crew, M., 5
Crocker, T., 8
Dales, J., 131
David, M., 147
Dead weight losses, 2, 19-22, 174
Derthick, M., 176, 182n
Ellis, L., 10n

Elmore, T., 159, 160
Emission charges, 138-146, 164-167
Emissions trading, 149-156
Faden, R., 192, 193
Fischhoff, B., 128n, 192
Foster, W., 197
Freeman, A., 203n
Graham, D., 192
Hahn, R., 134, 145-149, 156, 161, 165, 168-178, 181n
Hammond, P., 9
Harris, M., 192
Hazard warnings
    alcohol, 104-112
    food, 112-127
    principles of effective
    policy, 87-99
Hester, G., 149, 156, 165, 170, 172, 178, 181n
Holmstrom, B., 192
Huber, J., 91, 128n
Hueth, D., 200
Ilgen, T., 176
Informed consent, 190-202
Interest Group Pressure, 2-4, 16-22, 30-50, 173
Ippolito, P., 197
Jarrell, G., 21
Jasanoff, S., 176
Joeres, E., 147
Johnson, R., 141, 177, 180n

Just, R., 197, 200
Kahneman, D., 9, 195
Kashmanian, R., 160
Kneese, A., 131
Kneuper, R., 51n
Lave, L., 177
Lead trading, 157-159
Levine, M., 176
Loomes, G., 203n
MacLean, D., 194
McChesney, F., 31, 51n
McCubbins, M., 167
McGartland, A., 161, 181n
Maget, W., 6, 91, 128n
Marketable permits, 146-162, 164-167, 173
Martin, R., 51n
Millsaps, S., 10n
Monopoly, 5, 55-79
Montgomery, W., 134
Morrall, F., 129n
Neary, J., 199
Noll, R., 147, 173, 175
Novotny, G., 146, 148
Nowell, C., 4
Oates, W., 132
Olson, M., 2, 3, 22
O'Neil, W., 147
Opschoor, J., 176, 177, 181n
Overeynder, P., 160
Page, T., 167
Panzer, J., 5, 55, 58, 66, 79n
Partial regulation, 56-79
Patterson, D., 147, 148
Peltzman, S., 2, 21, 26n, 31, 46, 51n
Pigou, A., 131
Pittle, D., 88, 128n, 190
Plott, C., 1, 10n, 134
Posner, R., 31, 51n
Price, J., 51n
Proposition 65, 112-127
Quirk, P., 176, 182n
Ramsey pricing, 20, 58-62, 79n
Raviv, A., 192
Rent seeking, 30-51
Roberts, K., 195, 199
Rolph, E., 169
Sandman, P., 195
Sandmo, A., 9
Schmalensee, R., 192
Schmitz, A., 200
Schoemaker, P., 203n

Schultze, C., 131
Schwartz, D., 197
Separation Procedures, 73-77
Sherman, R., 5
Shuford, G., 51n
Shulstad, R., 197
Simon, H., 128n, 179
Slovic, P., 191, 192
Smith, A., 13-15, 25
Smith, V. K., 6, 9, 196
Spiller, P., 21
Sprenger, R., 137, 146
Stigler, G., 2, 31, 51n, 62, 128n
Stoevener, H., 197
Strand, I., 197
Sugden, R., 203n
Sustainability, 5, 58-73
Svenson, O., 192
Sweeney, G., 74
Thomas, L., 149
Tietenberg, T., 134, 181n
Tschirhart, J., 4, 79n
Tulluck, G., 2, 31, 51n, 135, 167
Tversky, A., 9, 195
Veatch, R., 193
Viscusi, W.K., 91, 128n, 129n, 192
Weinstein, M., 195
Welch, W., 169
Willig, R., 5, 55, 58, 59, 66, 79n
Yandle, B., 51n, 61
Young, E., 51n